GOD IN YOUR GOALS

Reconciling your spiritual journey
with success "in the world"

2nd Edition July 2015

Rick Seymour

Paperback ISBN: ISBN-13: 978-1495475276
                    ISBN-10: 1495475271

This book is dedicated to Aldona – my wife, my friend, my love, my constant encourager and supporter.

Foreword

Postscript
Afterword
After-Afterword

Foreword to the 2nd Edition July 2015

There has been an extraordinary amount of research done in the last handful of years on motivation and how the brain functions and processes information. With new technologies that allow us to literally "see" what is going on in the brain, scientists have been able to understand things that were merely wishful thinking a decade ago. Some of the concepts that I shared in the 1st edition are due to be updated and corrected in light of this new research – much of which is not only interesting, but exciting. I'm sure that if there are any major breakthroughs in the science in coming years a 3rd edition will be forthcoming, but for now this is the best we have.

FOREWORD

I come to this topic not as a religious scholar or theologian, but as a lay person, entrepreneur and businessman trying to reconcile my Christian walk with my business life. Early in my career as an entrepreneur I learned the value of having a solid vision, setting goals, creating strategic plans and activity plans, as well as many other skills that are considered to be mainstream in the secular business community. I studied social psychology at the graduate level, read tons of books on the psychology of the mind and spent thousands of dollars on "self-help" books.

But then several years ago I became very sensitized to anything smacking of the "humanistic" movement. Anyone talking about goals, affirmations, visualization, etc. was accused of being humanistic or "New Age" and immediately suspect in the Christian community. In fact, my wife and I became so gun-shy about the topic that we quit doing anything that could be remotely related to what the "New Agers" were doing. Over a period of a couple of years we saw our marriage begin to plateau and our business begin to plateau and in fact start to go downhill. It took a while to recognize that our lack of focus, lack of goal-setting and lack of working on ourselves was the cause for our lack of success in every arena of our lives – personal as well as business.

Unfortunately, the logic that led up to this sad state of affairs is not any different than to say: "Since the humanists drink milk, we as Christians had better not be caught drinking milk."

It finally dawned on me that these life skills were no different than any other that Satan has attempted to take ownership of. Satan takes God's truth and perverts it just enough to get people off track, leaving enough truth to mislead people into thinking that they really are OK.

After several years of frustration I decided it was time for me to get into God's Word and find out what HE has to say about all of this -- to see if I could discern the truth to be found in the real source of wisdom – the "manufacturer's handbook" -- the inspired word of

God – the Bible. We've all heard it said that there is "nothing new under the sun". Well, in this case that is certainly true. Any wisdom that you find in this book is not mine – it's been around for thousands of years in the Old and New Testament – I am merely the messenger. Virtually every concept that I put forward in this book I have provided the scriptural justification for. Whether or not you believe that the Bible is the inspired word of God, I urge you to accept the wisdom of what it has lent to this book.

I ended up spending an hour or two a day for the better part of two years doing a word search about all of the subjects found in this book. I practically wore out my Strong's Concordance (yes – that was before having on-line Bible searches readily available).

What I did discover was that in fact these are God-given truths and we will be OK utilizing these concepts as long as we maintain the right perspective. Hosea 4:6 says, "My people are destroyed for lack of knowledge…" Let us never be guilty of failing to fulfill our calling because of lack of knowledge.

Habakkuk 2:2-4 says, "And the Lord answered me and said, Write the vision and make it plain upon the tablets, that he who reads it may run. The vision awaits for its appointed time; it hastens to the end; it will not lie. Even if it seems slow, wait for it; it will certainly come, it will not delay. Behold, the wicked shall fail, but the righteous shall live by his faith." Seeking God's will for our lives, establishing God-centered goals and learning to live by vision and faith is the crux of this book. But let us not be so arrogant as to believe that it is all about us. Setting goals isn't just about what we want to do, but what we believe God can do through us to advance His kingdom!

We must continually seek God's will for our lives and set our goals accordingly. And we must make sufficient room for God to make a few adjustments. His vision for us does not change, it is not variable. But our life is a journey and our perception of God's vision for us may be clouded by doubt, ungodly thoughts or sin. These must be corrected. There will be adjustments to our course throughout our lives. But don't let that deter you from moving ahead. The sovereignty of God is no excuse for inactivity, procrastination, irresponsibility or laziness. God is much bigger than our mistakes. Wouldn't you rather be pursuing a God-centered goal that might need occasional course corrections, than to be doing nothing for the Kingdom out of fear that you might miss His will for your life?

It is time to act. It is time to change. It is time to grow into the person that God wants you to be. It is no longer acceptable to coast through life. Daniel 11:32 "....but the people that know their God shall stand firm and *take action*." Now is the time. My prayer is that this book may be one of the tools that help you grow in your spiritual, business and personal walk.

At the end of each chapter I have shared some others' insights that have read this book which will give you a slightly different perspective on the topic and hopefully, help you grow and change. I think it is a fun and fascinating journey. I am glad you are joining me.

Chapter 1
PERSPECTIVE

What is the right perspective for our lives? Most of us, Christian or not, strive to achieve some sort of balance in our lives -- balance between our working world, our family, other important relationships, and our spiritual lives. But what does balance really look like? For most it's a juggling act. But should it be?

Allow me to suggest some definitions for the "spiritual", "emotional" and "physical" parts of our lives. Very simply put, the spiritual part of our lives is our relationship with our creator. For our purposes, let's define our relationships – marriage, family, children, friends, etc. as the "emotional" part of our lives. The "physical" part of our lives is all the "stuff" – as in "He who dies with the most toys wins" type of "stuff". (However, please note that he who dies with the most toys, still dies!) It's what most peoples' working lives are about – how to get all the "stuff" – the big house, the luxury car, the boat, the country club membership...

The world's view of how to achieve balance among these three parts of our lives is limiting and difficult, if not impossible for anyone to achieve under their own power. Most people see the three major aspects of their lives as separate and distinct – the spiritual, the emotional and the physical.

It's as though they have three buckets of balls and the trick is to grab a ball from each bucket and start juggling them and keep them all in the air at once. When they get pretty good with three balls, they reach down and grab a fourth ball from one of the buckets and when they get pretty good at four, they reach for a ball from another bucket and when they get pretty good at keeping five balls in the air, they reach down for...

Well, if it is a juggling act, then disaster is waiting just around the corner, because eventually they are going to drop all of the balls. It's not a good way to find balance, because eventually it all falls apart.

I firmly believe that balance is an inside-out job. It is more like three concentric circles. On the inside is the spiritual, then the emotional and finally, the physical. You can have all the "stuff" in the world, but if your relationships are failing and you are not spiritually grounded, you will ultimately be miserable. We have all watched people that are so committed to their business or job that they sacrifice their families in the process of becoming "successful". The really unfortunate part is that in most cases they thought they were doing it for their families.

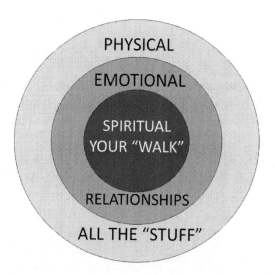

Without being spiritually grounded, it is difficult, if not impossible to have any long-term relationships provide real joy. We place too many expectations and too heavy a burden on others – especially our spouse - to 'make us happy.'

When Aldona and I met, we came from opposite ends of the world – both literally and figuratively. Aldona is Lithuanian. Her parents, her older sister and she escaped from Lithuania during World War II and ended up in a refugee camp in Munich, Germany. Aldona spent six of her first 10 years of life literally starving in that camp. Through a series of miracles that would take too long to explain, she and her parents and sister came to the United States on an Army troop ship through Ellis Island. They came with one suitcase, no money, didn't speak English and had a VERY conservative Roman Catholic, Eastern European value system.

When Aldona met me, I was the product of middle-class America in the 60's. An extremely liberal, long-haired, hippie freak – as well as a flaming atheist that would cut you off at the knees if you tried to talk "religion" to me. I had been on a "spiritual quest" -- into every occult thing you could imagine. How the two of us ever connected makes absolutely no sense, except to say that God must have an extraordinary sense of humor!

We both brought all the bills and all the baggage from our previous marriages into this one. Our first five years together were probably one of the rockiest starts to a marriage that there has ever been. In fact, I think Aldona wore out the hinges on three suitcases packing to leave about once a week!

So what changed? How is it that for the last 41 years we have had a marriage that is the envy of most people we know? In fact, we know only a small handful of couples that have a marriage as full, rewarding, loving and complete as we have. How did we get from where we were to where we are today? WE didn't. The Lord completed that work in us.

Early in the development of our business we had two associates – Lenard and Dori Funck. They lived down the canyon from us, in the mountains west of Denver. We had literally nothing in common other than our business relationship. But because they were on our way to and from town, we frequently were dropping something off to them either going or coming. The weird thing was that we would often find ourselves sitting in their kitchen for two to three hours at a time, without really having anything to talk about. It turns out in retrospect, that they had a peace in their home that we didn't have in ours. It was so soothing, so attractive, and so peaceful, that we just wanted to be there instead of our own home with all the problems, the tension, the conflict and the chaos.

I was still working as an aerospace engineer (Yes, I was a rocket scientist) while we were building our business part-time. I had worked with or around Lenard for six to seven years. He had been around enough "bull" sessions in the office to know that I became rabid whenever the topic of religion came up. As a consequence, neither he nor Dori ever brought up the subject of religion for the first couple of years that we visited in their kitchen, even though they were strong Christians and committed to their Christian walk because they knew that I would have reacted by severing the relationship if they had tried to talk 'religion' to me.

At the time, Aldona and I were really struggling financially. She was getting no support from her ex-husband and two-thirds of our combined incomes went to my ex-wife in the form of child-support, alimony and her college education. With two teenagers in our home, it was a real struggle. One evening we found ourselves sitting in Lenard and Dori's kitchen and Lenard said, "Say, there is a Full Gospel Business Men's Dinner up at the Desperado Restaurant Tuesday night. We'll buy your dinner if you would like to join us." At that point, Aldona and I had not had a meal out in a restaurant in months. The kids and we had been living on peanut butter and macaroni and cheese. We probably would have gone to a dog fight for a free meal. We said yes. It never registered on us what a Full Gospel Business Men's Dinner was – all we heard was, FREE MEAL. Len and Dori said they would pick us up on their way to the restaurant.

When we walked through the door of the restaurant there were all these people clapping their hands and praising the Lord. Aldona freaked out – with her conservative Roman Catholic upbringing. I freaked out – an avowed atheist had no business in a place like this. I looked at Aldona and said, "I know who these people are. They are those 'holy rollers' my mother warned me about!" But since we didn't drive, we couldn't leave. The meal was over, and before the program started, Lenard and Dori could sense how uncomfortable we were. Being very gracious, they asked us if we would like to leave and we said "YES!" None of us said a word on the way back home other than a "Thanks for dinner" as we slammed their car door. As we walked into the house I said to Aldona, "Not again in a million years!"

A month goes by. We find ourselves one more time, sitting in Len and Dori's kitchen. Len says, "There's another Full Gospel Business Men's Dinner Tuesday night. We'll buy your dinner if you would like to join us." Out of our mouths at the same time came, "Sure." Immediately we realized the mistake we had made, but were too embarrassed to back out. I recovered quickly enough however, to say that we would drive ourselves this time (thinking that we would just eat and leave like we had the last time).

That Tuesday evening we walked in the door of the restaurant and all the same shenanigans were going on as before. We both locked up as we sat down to dinner. When the meal was over, both of us were uncomfortable about leaving, since this was the second free meal that we prevailed upon Lenard and Dori for. To this day neither Aldona nor I can tell you who spoke or what they talked about. All we know is that at the end of the program there was an altar call. I didn't want to go up front. I had no intention of going up front. All I wanted was to get out of there. But it was as though a giant hand pushed me out my seat and the next thing I knew I was standing at the front of the room accepting Jesus Christ as my Lord and Savior – and Aldona was right next to me.

That was the beginning of the healing of our marriage, the beginning of our understanding the source of true joy in our lives, the beginning of basing our marriage upon Biblical principles.

Do you know couples that think it is their spouse's responsibility to make them happy? That is a heavy burden to put upon anyone. Not only that, but when we place those kinds of expectations on someone else, we are setting ourselves up for disappointment. No matter how caring, how loving, how altruistic any of us would like to be, because of our fallen state, we are inherently selfish. All of us have areas of our lives that we are unwilling to change or give up or to which we are blind.

The only place that we can expect true perfection in this life is in our relationship with Jesus Christ. And that perfection is a one-way street – Christ is perfect -- we can't give it, we can merely receive Christ's perfection and His grace. That is our only source of true and everlasting joy. So, knowing that, when we quit putting unrealistic expectations on our spouse, we take the pressure off the relationship and it can begin to work according to God's principles. Jesus Christ is the perfect third partner in a marriage.

As we developed a Christ-centered marriage, we came to understand that true love is not just some mushy-gushy feeling that we have for a time and then later on when we don't feel mushy and gushy we think, "We're just not in love any more." Love is not just a feeling. Love is a choice. Love is a decision. Love is how we choose to treat another person, regardless of our feelings at the moment.

In 1 Corinthians 13 it says: Love is patient. Love is kind. Love is not jealous or boastful. Love is not arrogant or rude. Love is not self-seeking or arrogant or resentful. Love is not easily provoked. Love does not rejoice at injustice, but rejoices in the truth. Love bears all things. Love believes all things. Love hopes all things. Love endures all things. Love never fails.

There is nothing in those verses about love being a "feeling." Those verses are a prescription for how we are to treat another person that we profess to love. It is about behavior. It is about our actions toward another. And when we choose to treat another person as described in 1 Corinthians, feelings of love follow and are reciprocated by the other person. Most people have it backwards. They wait until they **"feel"** love, before they are willing to treat the other person **with** love. The consequence of that approach is a downward spiral. If they don't "feel" loving, they don't treat their spouse in loving ways. Their spouse, not feeling loved, responds in unloving ways, resulting in even fewer "feelings" of love – and around and around it goes – and where it stops, everyone knows – divorce. That is exactly where Aldona and I were headed until we put Christ and God's word in the middle of our marriage.

We had finally come to the realization that until we were grounded spiritually, our marriage would never function properly. And when our relationship wasn't working, all the "stuff" in the world could never satisfy us. That is why it truly is an "inside-out job." Grounded by our spiritual walk first, our relationship second, and then when all of that is right, the "stuff" is a lot of fun.

But let's get to the real focus of this book: How do we reconcile our Christian walk with our daily toils to get ahead in the world? First, as we work toward "success" in the secular world, let us always be mindful of staying in God's will. But secondly, we also need to realize that our work and our ministry do not have to be two separate things when we are truly living for the Lord. I used to think that I had my job, my business, my profession – and then outside of that I had my ministry. It never really occurred to me that the two could be integrated. We've all heard the old saying, "Grow where you're planted." I think we can also say, "Minister where you're planted." We should all "minister in the marketplace." A committed, successful, ethical, hard-working person engaged in ANY endeavor "who does everything as unto the Lord", is a powerful witness to others. We do not have to go "into ministry" to minister. The vast majority of Christians will never be in a professional ministry – but that should never prevent us from being a witness and an example to others through our work.

INSIGHTS: "It's an inside out job. None of it really matters if you are not spiritually grounded."

"God needs to be 1st in all of our relationships both personal & business."

"Love is a decision not a feeling. Keeping Christ as the center will permeate through the rest of my life."

Chapter 2
THREE REALITIES

You will be learning six basic laws that affect your behavior. Even though we will be focusing on how to reconcile our jobs, our businesses and our "success" orientation with our Christian walk, be assured that these laws apply to every area of your life. They apply just as well to your spiritual life and your relationships as they do to the physical and material aspects of life.

If you are married, do you think there might be something you could do in the next 90 days that would make your marriage dramatically worse? Of course there is. Do you think there is something you could do in the next 90 days that would make your marriage better? I'm sure you could think of something! Do you think there is something you could do in the next 90 days that would make your job or business dramatically worse? Of course there is. Do you think there is something you could do in the next 90 days that could make your job or business better? You bet. Do you think there is something you could do in the next 90 days that would make your walk with the Lord dramatically worse? I'm sure you could easily come up with something. Do you think there is something you could do in the next 90 days that would make your walk with the Lord better? No doubt.

The point of all these questions is quite simple: *Whether your future gets better or worse is YOUR CHOICE!* So, the first reality we have to face, is that our future is very dependent upon the choices we make. Have you been making the kind of choices that will lead you to your better future? Or, are there some choices you have been making that you need to change? Our circumstances, where we are in our lives right now is a consequence of the choices we have made up until today. That means WE ARE RESPONSIBLE. It is not someone else's fault. It's time to quit blaming your parents, your upbringing, your teachers, the economy or anything else. YOUR FUTURE WILL ALSO BE YOUR FAULT. That's actually an exciting thought because we can choose to make it better!

Start by __Choosing__ Your Attitude

One of the most important lessons that I ever learned in my life, I learned from a poster not a person. Early in my career as an entrepreneur (while still working full-time as an aerospace engineer) it was glaringly apparent that I lacked any people skills. That seems to go with the territory when you are an engineer. (By the way, do you know how to tell an introverted engineer from an extroverted engineer? When you are talking to an introverted engineer he is always looking down at his shoes. When you are talking to an extroverted engineer, he is looking down at your shoes.) Even though we were struggling financially, Aldona and I decided it was important for me to take a course at the local community college on 'selling'. It turned out to be the worst course I have ever taken in my life. It was taught by a gentleman that had spent his whole life in academia. He had never sold anything to anyone out in the business world. It was a lot of boring, theoretical claptrap that had nothing to do with the real world. I stuck it out for the whole 12 weeks, because I didn't want the family to feel bad that we had 'wasted' the money on tuition. I sat in the same spot, in the same desk every week for 12 weeks, staring at the same poster on the wall for two hours.

All the poster said was, **"To be enthusiastic, you must act enthusiastic."** The first couple of weeks that I read it I thought, "That's not true. How can you be enthusiastic if you don't feel like it?" By about the fourth week I started to wonder if that could actually be true. About half way through the class I decided that there just might be an element of truth attached to that statement, so I decided to try it out. I decided that I would act enthusiastic and see what might happen.

At the time I was still working around lots of other engineers and had not yet made the transition to being full-time in my own business. When I was walking down the hall and somebody asked, "How are you?" I began responding with one of two things. I would either say, "If I were any better I'd need to be twins, just to spread it around a little bit!!!" Or I would say, "I'm terrific, but I'm going to get better!!!"

You can imagine the kind of responses I got when I started doing this – especially from a bunch of engineers. They all wondered what I had been smoking! Think about how most other people respond to you when you ask them how they are. I'll bet that you get a lot of what I call "contingent" answers: "Oh, I'm OK for a Monday." "I'd be better if it were Friday." "I'm great. It's payday!" "Pretty good for this early in the morning." "I'm doing pretty well under the circumstances." Do any of those sound familiar?

Most people respond based upon the circumstances. But, what I found when I started responding (<u>acting - choosing</u>) enthusiastically, was that almost immediately, I felt enthusiastic. The poster was right! "To be enthusiastic, you must act enthusiastic." The most important lesson that I learned was that the feelings follow the behavior, not the other way around. Every day we get to choose our attitude by how we choose to behave. It's very difficult to behave one way and feel another. **So choose to act enthusiastic.**

I found after a very few days of "acting enthusiastic", not only did it work for me, but it started to affect the people around me. Someone would see me walking down the hall and get a big grin on their face because they could hardly wait to ask me how I was – they knew it would be one of the few positive things they would hear all day. I could walk into the "bullpen" where I worked and I could see the energy level pick up a bit because things were just better when "ol'

Rick is here." People that are excited and enthusiastic about life naturally attract others.

Of course there are exceptions to everything. There was one guy named Ray that I worked with. Every time he asked how I was and I responded with one of my enthusiastic answers, I could see him lock up. It really annoyed him. He was a pretty bright guy and it only took him a couple days to figure out that if he didn't ask me how I was, he wouldn't have to listen to my "goofy" answer. For several weeks he would just pass me in the hall and totally ignore me. He wouldn't make eye contact. He would just act like I wasn't there.

One morning, after a few weeks, Ray turned the corner in hallway, glanced up and started to say, "Mornin'. How are......" before he realized that it was me. But it was too late. I answered him with, "If I were any better I'd need to be twins, just to spread it around a little." He locked up, made a U-turn in the hallway and followed me the whole length of the engineering building. I stepped on the elevator and he followed me. The elevator door closed and Ray turned around and got right in my face. He said, "That's #@!* it! Nobody is that good all the time! You are lying!!!!!" I thought about it for a moment and I said, "Ray I am not lying. I am merely telling the truth in advance." Remember, the behavior precedes the feelings.

I know some of you are thinking, "Well, if you had everything going on in your life that I have going on in mine, you wouldn't be enthusiastic and positive either." Then you miss the point. Attitude is a choice -- It is 5% what happens to you and 95% how you choose to respond.

I was listening to the radio one morning and heard someone describing his 84-year-old mother. She lives on her own, by herself, in a small town in Vermont. All three of her kids (including the one speaking on the radio) live in the same town. At least once a day, at least one of the kids checks in on her. One day in the late fall she was walking down her long gravel driveway to her mailbox. On her way back to the house, she stumbled, fell into the ditch and broke her hip. She lay there for four and a half hours before her son stopped by on his way home from work and found her. He called 911 and got her to the hospital.

The next morning he was visiting her in the hospital and this is the conversation he described... He said to his mother, "Mom, weren't you scared laying there with a broken hip for four and a half hours?" She said, "Not at all. I knew one of you kids would be by." Then he said, "Well, you must have been in an awful lot of pain!" His mom said, "Son, when I fell, I landed right in this pile of leaves, and they smelled sooooo gooood!" Finally he said, "Well, you must have been freezing because all you had on was a light sweater!" She responded, "You know, every once in a while the sun would come out from behind a cloud and I don't think I've ever appreciated sunshine as much as I did yesterday." There was nothing he could say that would bring her down. Do you think that is because she 'felt' that way? Or do you think that is because that is the way she <u>decided</u> to live her life? It's all about the choices we make every day of our lives.

The next time you hear someone say, "I'm doing pretty well under the circumstances." why don't you ask them what Zig Ziglar always asked, "Well, what are you doing under there anyway?"

It all comes down to the fact that to be in control of your life and your future you must recognize that feelings follow the behavior. Most people live their lives letting their behavior be determined by their feelings and as a consequence nothing ever changes.

Most people live their lives backward...

HAVE – DO – BE is the order that most people think life happens. They think it looks like this:

"When I *HAVE* more money I will be able to *DO* the things I want to do and then I will *BE* happy" or

"When I *HAVE* more time I will be able to *DO* all the things I want for my kids and then I can *BE* a better Dad."

But instead **BE – DO – HAVE** is how it really works. For example:

"Who do I need to *BE* so that I will *DO* the things I need to do in order to *HAVE* the resources that will help me achieve my goals?"

"Who do I need to *BE* so that I will *DO* the things I need to do in order to *HAVE* the time I want to spend with my kids?"

Once again it is your behavior that precedes the desired outcome. Look at it this way: Think of two or three of your greatest successes in the last year. How would you describe your 'state of *BEING*' during those times? Check any of those below that fit (and add any others that aren't on the list that would describe you)

What 'states of being' would describe your successes?

- ☐ Passionate
- ☒ Enthusiastic
- ☒ Committed
- ☐ Taking responsibility
- ☒ Adventurous
- ☐ Risk-taking
- ☐ Accountable
- ☐ Out of comfort zone
- ☐ Trusting
- ☐ _____
- ☐ _____

Now think of two or three of your greatest disappointments of the last year. How would you describe your 'state of *BEING*' during those times?

What 'states of being' would describe your disappointments?

- ☐ Timid
- ☐ Fearful
- ☐ Pessimistic
- ☐ Blame
- ☐ Cautious
- ☐ Detached
- ☐ Frustrated
- ☐ Closed
- ☐ Cynical
- ☐ _____
- ☐ _____

From the first set of characteristics, which of those would you say you need to *BE*come **more of**? From the second list which of those characteristics would you say you need to *BE*come **less of**? Make a note of that as you begin to figure out how to change your 'state of *BE*ing'.

INSIGHTS: "We must consciously **CHOOSE** our behavior and our attitude."

"It is our responsibility of what our lives can be."

"My attitude should reflect Christ and his transforming power in my life."

"Be MORE: Accountable, Committed, Out of comfort zone...Be LESS: Fearful, Cautious, Timid....Your attitude is a choice."

"Attitude is a choice. Start TODAY choosing the attitude that you will need in order to have the life you want."

CHAPTER 3
Your NON-Conscious Mind
Is Driving Your Bus

There is a subtle trap...
There are two parts of our mind that are functioning all the time – the conscious mind and the subconscious mind (or NONconscious mind might be a better way to describe it). The trap is that 90% of the choices/decisions we make are made non-consciously without us even recognizing how or why. Think of it like an iceberg: The 90% that you can't see or even be aware of is your non-conscious mind. That means <u>90% of the "choices" we make we have no choice about</u>.

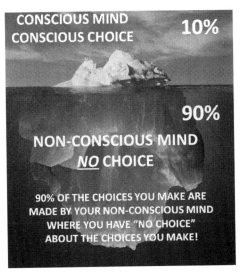

The only way to improve the 90% is to alter/improve what resides in our non-conscious mind. We will be coming back to this in a later chapter because it is crucial to our personal growth. Understand that "We see things the way we are, not the way they are!"

OK, So We Need To Make Better Choices Every Day

If we recognize that we need to change, what will motivate us to change? – Especially knowing that most of us find change uncomfortable and resist even the smallest changes in our lives.

Let's get real for a minute. Is the toilet paper supposed to roll from the top of the roll or the bottom of the roll? Whatever it is for you, you know that this is "the way it is supposed to be." If it is not put on "properly", it tends to set us off and grumble about whoever it was that put it on last – assuming you can even get them to replace an empty roll! In fact, I know people for whom this tiny little change in their life upsets them so much, that as a guest in someone else's home they will turn it around! Yep, I've done it. If that little bit of change sets people off, what do you suppose trying to make really big changes in your life does to you?

The only reason we would ever suffer the discomfort of change, is because we have a good enough reason to change. We have to know WHY it is important to change. In fact, **without an adequate answer to the question "Why?"** <u>**ANY**</u> **price is too high to pay!** None of us will go through the discomfort of change without sufficient justification. Until we are convinced of the **need** to change, we will not even begin the attempt.

Suppose We Know WHAT. Suppose We Know WHY.
Now The Question Is HOW To Change.

If we recognize that we need to make better choices, if we recognize WHY we need to change – the question then becomes – HOW do we change? That is what the bulk of this book is about. The choices we make are a function of how we think. So to make different choices, we have to have different thinking. Thus, *the quality of our future will depend upon the quality of our thinking.* The rest of this book will teach you how to change your thinking.

In summary, the three realities that we have to come to grips with are:

> 1) Whether our future gets better or worse is our **choice**.
> 2) Without an adequate answer to the question **"Why?"** **ANY price is too high to pay** to change.
> 3) The quality of our future depends upon the **quality of our thinking**.

By changing our thinking, we can change our lives. Your mind is a powerful thing. No it is not as powerful as God, no it can't make you like God or become God. (Although there are some people that believe that.) However, it is amazing what your mind is capable of even wehn chaglelend wtih seomtnhig new and unmfaliair, if you are oepn to it. Aoccdrnig to a rscheearch at Cmabrigde Uinervtisy, it deosn't mttaer in waht oredr the ltteers in a wrod are, the olny iprmoatnt tihng is taht the frist and lsat ltteer be in the rghit pclae. The rset can be a taotl mses and you can sitll raed it wouthit a porbelm. Tihs is bcuseae the huamn mnid deos not raed ervey lteter by istlef, but the wrod as a wlohe. Amzanig huh? yaeh and I a wlyas tghuhot slpeling was ipmorantt!

See how quickly, with no explanation at all your mind adapted to something so different and unusual? Your mind is capable of doing extraordinary things. We will spend several chapters learning how to harness that power and turn it towards our good instead of continually sabotaging ourselves.

But for the balance of this book, if you find any real typos that I didn't catch, I'll rely on Mark Twain who said: "I've got no respect for any person that can't spell a word more than one way." ☺

THREE GOOD QUESTIONS

The First good question: What will you do to survive?

I'm talking about elemental, gut-level survival. I'm talking about my wife, Aldona, six years old in a refugee camp in Munich, Germany. I'm NOT talking about whether you can pay the mortgage and the credit card bills this month. I am talking about you starving, your kids starving and you have no food, no friends, no money and no credit. Your neighbor has bread, but won't give you any. What will you do? Remember your kids are starving. What will you do? You know stealing is wrong, but what will you do? Stealing violates your ethical standards. But your kids are starving, what will you do? Will you let your kids starve? My guess is, you will do WHATEVER IT TAKES. And isn't that the essence of how we're wired: We will do whatever it takes to survive!

The Second good question: What will you do to succeed?

Most people would immediately say: "WHATEVER IT TAKES!" But, wouldn't you agree that if that were true, we'd all be further along in our lives right now? And I'm not talking about violating your ethical standards. Within the confines of what is right, ethical and legal have you done whatever it takes to succeed? Have you done everything you know you could do? Probably not.

That leads us to ***the third good question: "Why haven't you done everything you could do to succeed?"*** By the time you finish the next couple of chapters, you will know the answer to that question. In the meantime, let me give you a hint.

For those of you that are gardeners, I would like you to think about what would happen if you were to plant your garden in the spring and then not check in until fall. Obviously, you would have a plot of weeds and you would never reap much of a harvest – if any. You could pretend that the weeds aren't there; you could do lots of positive affirmations about how bountiful your garden is; you could visualize lots of wonderful produce or you could even go out and curse the weeds. But you would still have weeds. I have a news flash for you – we all have some weeds in our garden (in our non-conscious mind). Unless we are willing to acknowledge the weeds and do something about them, we will never see the bounty of what we would like to harvest in our lives. The first half of this book will show you how to recognize the weeds in your garden. The second half will show you how to get rid of them.

Let me caution you. As you read this book, please stay on "Channel 1". Stay focused on you. I'm sure there will be many times that you will be thinking to yourself, "Boy I wish so-and-so would read this." Well, they're not reading it (yet). If you spend all your time fussing over who else should be getting this stuff, you will miss some important lessons for yourself. When you have finished reading the book, you can go and invest what you have learned in someone else's life. But until then, stay on "Channel 1!"

INSIGHTS: "90% of the choices we make we have no choice about." *"We see the world the way we are, not the way it is."*
"My life is so controlled by the 90% of my nonconscious brain."
"You need a WHY!"

CHAPTER 4
WHAT DO YOU THINK?

As we were growing up, most of us were taught WHAT to think, but most of us were never taught HOW to think. Why is that a problem? Consider this:

For every 100 Americans at age 65:
1 will be wealthy
4 will be financially independent
32 will be dead (they never learned how to take care of themselves - or ignored good advice)
63 will be dead broke (hoping Social Security or their family will bail them out)

We usually focus on the top two categories, but for a moment I want you to focus on the bottom two categories where 95% of the people never figure it out!

As you were growing up, your parents were the first ones that taught you how the world worked. Then your teachers were telling you how the world worked. Next your bosses on the job were telling you how the world worked. What are the odds that some of what you were taught and what you believe will get you ahead in the world is wrong? – About 95%! We got a lot of bad information, but if we believe that information is true, and behave as though it is true – we will probably end up like the 95%! It is almost a certainty.

Our limiting thoughts are what keep us where we are. There is a real, **physiological** reason as to why that is true (not just a psychological reason), and we will address it in a later chapter when we talk about the Reticular Activating System (RAS). But for now, let me give you a couple of examples.

BREAKING THE BARRIER

Roger Bannister broke the 4-minute mile barrier on May 6, 1954. It was called the "greatest athletic achievement of all time". Prior to Roger Bannister breaking the 4-minute barrier it was thought humanly impossible to accomplish such a feat. In fact doctors and physiologists of the day said that it would exceed the capacity of the human heart to perform. They believed the heart would give out and you would die if you ever pushed your body to that level of effort.

If you believed that were true and you were the star miler on your college track team, and you had trained to the maximum for an upcoming event, what might happen? Suppose as you finish your first lap you hear your coach yell. "59.8!!!" After you finish your second lap, you hear your coach yell, "59.9!!!" After your third lap you hear your coach yell, "59.9!!!!!!" How long will it take you to run the fourth lap? At least 60.5 seconds. Why? Because you know that if you keep up this pace, your heart is going to give out and you are going to die! So, nonconsciously you back off just enough, that when you finish you hear, "4:01!" and you think, "Way to go, you are awesome!" But is there a possibility that you could have broken four minutes? Probably. Was it your legs, your heart or your lungs that kept you from doing it? Maybe not. It more than likely was your thinking, your belief system that held you back.

But then, Roger Banister had the unmitigated gall to break the 4-minute barrier – and not die. Isn't it interesting that within six weeks John Landy broke Bannister's record and within one year 5 other runners broke the 4-minute barrier? Do you think it was just a rather fortuitous alignment of the stars, that in that particular year, seven runners broke the 4-minute barrier? Or could it be that once people thought it was possible (without dying), they could go out and do it. Today the record stands at 3:43:13. Any middle-distance runner today that can't run a sub-four-minute mile, might as well not even compete. Today, in world-class competition it is the expectation – the price of entry – the norm.

FLAT WORLD THINKING

What was going on in the world in 1491? We all know what happened in 1492 – "Columbus sailed the ocean blue." But more importantly, what was going on in 1491? Columbus was preparing to sail around the world. The interesting thing about it was that he lived in a world of 'flat world' thinkers (at least 95% of them! – Proverbs 23:7 "As a man thinketh in his heart (his non-conscious mind) so is he." – If you think the world is flat, you will act as though the world is flat). The first thing Columbus had to do was raise the money to build the ships. Can you imagine him going to the bankers to get a loan? (Would you agree that bankers are by-and-large a rather conservative bunch?) So here is Columbus trying to sell the bankers on the idea and the bankers are saying, "You want to do WHAT?! You're going to take these ships, you'll sail off the edge of the earth and I'll lose my investment. Forget it!"

Columbus finally convinces Queen Isabella to finance the deal. Now he has to raise a crew -- from flat-world thinkers. What kind of response do you suppose he got from that? "Are you nuts? I'm not going to go out there and sail off the edge of the earth!" (That was the 95%...) And you think you have a tough sell in your business? Most of us will only operate within the confines of what we think is possible. Until our thinking changes, we can't see ourselves 'breaking the barrier' or 'sailing around the world' or closing that really big deal or having that really terrific relationship.

"We see things the way we are, not the way they are!"

BAD MAPS

Suppose you are driving around Denver, Colorado looking for a certain address where you are supposed to be for a meeting at 8:00 AM, but you can't find it. You got up early. You were excited. You were motivated. You were self-disciplined. You really wanted to reach your destination, your "goal". You don't understand why you can't get there because you have this incredibly detailed map. It is very accurate, it was developed with satellite photography, and has every building on it. No important detail is left out. But you can't find where you want to go. You finally give up in frustration and go back home.

You take the map in the house with you because you want to study it and figure out where you went wrong. As you are sitting at the kitchen table looking at the map, you notice down in the lower right-hand corner, it says "Dallas, Texas". What was the problem? You had the wrong map. You were excited. You were motivated. You were self-disciplined. You really wanted to reach the goal, but you couldn't. Would it have turned out differently if you had had the right map? Of course it would.

What you may discover as you progress through this book is that about 95% of the "maps" that you are using to navigate through this world and achieve "success" are wrong (a few of the weeds in your garden if you will...). There is nothing wrong with you, you just have some bad maps.

The "territory" itself does not change, regardless of how accurate your map is. You need to discover which of your maps are bad and replace them with good ones. Some of your thinking needs to change before you can begin to achieve new goals! (Perhaps even 95% of your thinking needs to change.) "We see things the way we are, not the way they are!"

I don't ever remember when I was growing up being taught HOW to think, only WHAT to think. But until we know HOW we think, there is no way to change WHAT we think and it is WHAT we think that keeps us stuck in our lives. Remember, the quality of our future will depend upon the quality of our thinking. So, I guess it's time that we learned HOW we think.

THE 'OZ' CODE

Let me share a wonderful story with you that you already know – or at least think you know. The "Wizard of Oz". (Yes, I know some of you think this is a movie about two women fighting over a pair of shoes, but...) Those of you that are parents or grandparents of children under 13, let me encourage you to sit with them at least once a year and watch the movie. Afterwards, talk about it and what it means. Let me give you my version: Dorothy and Toto are lost in the Land of Oz. They discover that the only way they can get back home to Kansas is to follow the Yellow Brick Road to the Emerald City and find the Wizard. The wizard is the one that can save them.

Along the way they come across, what in today's terminology we would call, three "dysfunctional" people. (I have a real problem with that term because the word "dysfunctional" implies that someone else "did it to us." In other words, we have no responsibility for where we are in our lives – aaaah..., but that's a whole other book – maybe someday...) So, we have these three 'dysfunctional' folks. We have the scarecrow, who has no brain. There is the tin man, who has no heart. And finally, we have the lion that has no courage. They are headed down the Yellow Brick Road with Dorothy and Toto so that they can find the Wizard, because the Wizard is the one that can 'fix them'. They have to jump through a few hoops, kill the occasional witch, etc., before the Wizard finally agrees to 'fix them'.

The Wizard says to the scarecrow, "It's not that you don't have a brain. It's just that you don't have a diploma to prove it." So the Wizard gives the scarecrow a diploma and instantly the scarecrow is "fixed."

The Wizard says to the tin man, "It's not that you don't have a heart. It's just that you can't hear it ticking away down there." So he gives the tin man a clock that goes 'tick, tick, tick' and immediately he is "fixed".

Lastly, he looks at the lion and says, "It's not that you don't have any courage. It's that you don't have a medal to prove how brave you are. Here is your medal." And just like that the lion is 'fixed.' Wasn't that easy? You've got to love this story!

But, what do they then find out about the Wizard? The Wizard is a fake ---- **But they're still "fixed"!** So what was it that the Wizard really did? He changed their thinking. The minute they thought differently about themselves, they were fixed. I'm here to tell you that as soon as you change your thinking – as soon as you start to think differently about yourself – you too will begin to be 'fixed'. That's the good news! Now all we have to do is figure out HOW to change our thinking. Hold on tight!

INSIGHTS: "To change our lives we have to change our thoughts."

"The nonconscious thinking that controls me is still separated from the core of my forgiven Christ-centered being."

"The problem is between your ears."

"Think about a time where you had "flat world thing". What did it take for you to experience a true New World Breakthrough? This week keep a log of the times you wonder if things are impossible. What needs to change in your thinking?"

"The mind that thinks there is a limitation is the limitation."

Chapter 5
WHAT DO YOU THINK ABOUT?

I am going to identify six laws that affect your behavior. They have been working in your life since the day you were born. It doesn't matter whether you knew about them, understood them or could even explain them to someone else – they have still been working in your life. Unfortunately, they have been working against you 95% of the time, because you didn't know about them. But your ignorance of the laws does not prevent them from working in your life.

When you were two years old, did you know about, understand and have the ability to explain the law of gravity to someone else? Of course not. Did that mean you woke up in the morning sleeping on the ceiling? No. Your lack of awareness did not prevent the law of gravity from working in your life. These six laws are no different. Ignorant of them or not, they still work in your life. Your good intentions won't prevent them from working either. If someone had pushed Mother Theresa off the edge of a 30-story building, what would have happened? She would have fallen, obviously. You may think, "But she was a saint, she was one of the most extraordinary women the world has ever seen; she was the most gracious, most caring, most giving person on the planet – that's just not fair." It's not about fair, it's about the law – the law of gravity works for everyone, every time.

ALL six laws that effect your behavior work for everyone, every time. It doesn't matter whether you are good or bad, motivated or lazy or excited or bored about life. If you don't understand them or know about them, there is a very high probability that they have been working against you 95% of the time – but they have been working.

So, here is the first law that affects your behavior:

THE FIRST LAW

 What you *THINK ABOUT* affects you
What you *PUT* in your mind affects you
What you *ALLOW* into your mind affects you
What you *EXPOSE* your mind to affects you

DON'T DROP YOUR ARM! What do you *PUT* into your mind?

The best way to prove this to you is to demonstrate it physically. That's difficult to do in a book, but I will describe an experiment to you that has never failed in over 250 seminars, including one with a winner of the Mr. Universe competition.

I always ask for two volunteers – a man and a woman – folks that work out using weights and/or machines and have some upper-body strength (I try to find the burliest looking man and the most petite woman I can). I bring them to the front of the room and have them face the audience. I first test their upper-body strength to get a baseline. With the man, I have him hold his strongest arm straight out to his side with his palm down. I then push down at his wrist and have him resist me and try to keep from dropping his arm to his side. With the woman (since they have different muscle structure than men) I have her hold her strongest arm straight out to the side with her palm facing up. I place one hand inside her elbow and the other below the wrist and I try to bend her arm at the elbow and have her resist me.

Once we have established the strength baseline we do three different tests.

In the first test I ask each of them to close their eyes and think of some really negative thing that has happened to them in their lives. It could be their most embarrassing moment, the death of a loved one, or anything else they choose. They don't share it or verbalize it. They keep it all to themselves. Once they have thought of something, they hold out their arm and I ask them to continue to dwell on the negative event and ask when they are ready. We test their strength and what we invariably find is that they are significantly weaker than the baseline. Next, I ask each of them to keep their eyes closed and think about something really positive, exciting and fun in their lives and we test their strength again. They will always be dramatically stronger when thinking of something positive, than when thinking of something negative. The key here is that they **PUT** those thoughts into their minds themselves; I had nothing to do with their specific choices and they never shared them. It affects the strength of their arm and yet when I ask them afterwards whether or not they were thinking about their arm, the answer is always no.

But the thing to realize is that whether you are thinking about positive or negative things does not affect just the strength of your arm – it affects every area of performance in your life! You will be "stronger" when you are thinking about positive things than when you are thinking about negative things.

In the second test we do, I describe a scene and ask the subject to put themselves in the picture. For the man I say, "OK, close your eyes. This time do not drop your arm. No matter what I do, don't drop your arm. The goal is to not drop your arm! No matter what I do, do not drop your arm. I don't care if I do a chin-up on it, don't drop it! I don't care if I ask someone to come up here and help me, don't drop it! Remember, do not drop your arm! Remember, the goal of this exercise is DO NOT DROP YOUR ARM! So, when you are ready to not drop your arm, let me know." When they indicate they are ready, we test their strength. They will always be dramatically weaker than the baseline.

Next I say to them, "OK, close your eyes. Hold out your arm. This time we have a steel rod that is three inches in diameter. It is made for holding up bridges and buildings. It is incredibly strong. It is welded to an I-beam in the wall on your left and it runs through this shoulder, this other shoulder, through your arm and wrist and is welded to an I-beam on the other side of the room. (I run my hand across their shoulders and along their arm and wrist as I describe it) Got the picture? Tell me when you are ready." They are always dramatically stronger, and many times I can't get their arm all the way down to their side. What was the difference? In the first scenario *they* *were thinking about what they didn't want instead of what they did* *want*. I said over and over again, "Don't drop your arm!" In the second scenario they were thinking about what they did want – "Power and Strength" - and that is what they got.

The nonconscious mind does not respond to a negative, it only responds to the positive attribute of what you are describing or thinking about. Let me give you a couple of examples. Right now, DO NOT THINK ABOUT A PINK ELEPHANT! What image immediately popped into your mind, even though I told you not to? Right now, DO NOT THINK ABOUT A DOG CHASING A CAT! What image immediately popped into your mind? To tell yourself or someone else to NOT do something, merely puts that very image into their mind. When I say, "Don't drop your arm!" what image is your mind focused on? Dropping the arm. How many times have we told someone else, **"Now don't forget"**? What do you suppose their nonconscious mind is focused on? **Forgetting.**

On the other hand when we talk about what we do want -- steel rods, power and strength (and I only had to say it once – not repeat it over and over again), the subject was very strong. Wouldn't it make more sense that instead of reminding someone "Don't forget", we should be saying **"Now remember"**?

How often have we told a misbehaving child to go to their room and "Think about what you just did!"? Aren't we just reinforcing the behavior we DON'T want? Perhaps, "Go to your room and think about how you know you should treat your sister" would make more sense. We always need to describe and think about what it is we want, not what we don't want or are trying to get away from. If all we ever think about is the stack of bills on the desk, what do you suppose we get more of? Bills. Instead, we need to be thinking about abundance and having more than enough.

What Do You *Allow* Into Your Mind?

For the second test with the woman, I first describe a scene I know she'll hate and ask her to put herself in it: "Close your eyes. You now weigh 50 pounds more. You haven't worked out in months. You are out of shape. You have no energy. You have been eating nothing but junk food for weeks. You are finally so disgusted with yourself that you can't stand it anymore. It is your first day back at the health club. You have finished your workout. You decide to go to the Jacuzzi. You put on the same bathing suit you used to wear when you were 50 pounds lighter. You are watching the other people watch you, and thinking about what they are thinking about you. Got the picture? Tell me when you are ready." Usually you can watch them wilt right in front of you and they are incredibly weak when you bend their arm.

Next, I ask them to put themselves in this scene: "You are now at your ideal weight. You have been working out four times a week for the last year. You have been eating healthy foods consistently. You are strong. You are fit. You are toned. You have never felt better in your life. You are in the same bathing suit, walking to the same Jacuzzi, watching the same people watch you and are thinking about what they are thinking about you. Got the picture? Tell me when you are ready." More often than not, I can't even begin to bend their arm! So again, if we are thinking about what it is we don't want – we are very weak. But, if we will focus on what we do want – we are very strong – in every area of performance, not just our arms. The thing to remember especially is that both of the subjects **ALLOWED** me to put the scene into their minds.

What Do You *Expose* Your Mind To?

For the third test, I ask the subjects to face the front of the room so that they cannot see the audience and to keep their eyes shut through the whole thing. I coach the audience that when I give them the "thumbs up", I want them to think strong, positive thoughts about each of the subjects. When I give them the "thumbs down", I want them to think weak, negative things about each of the subjects. I ask the subjects to keep their eyes closed and to hold out their arms. I then give the audience the thumbs down. The subjects are always very weak when the audience is thinking negative things about them. The next time I say, "OK, this time let's do this..." And give the audience the thumbs down again. And again the subjects are very weak. The last time I say, "OK, this time let's..." and give the audience the thumbs up. And sure enough, the subjects are dramatically stronger. It's not unusual for them to be stronger than any other time we've tested them. Considering by now their arms should be ready to fall off, since we've done this seven times before, it's pretty eye-opening to see how strong they are on this last test!

I don't even begin to understand why this works, I just know that it works. Have you ever walked into a room of people and said to yourself, "Boy, there are really some bad vibes in here."? That's what we are talking about. You can sense this sort of thing. On the other hand, I'm sure you've walked into a room full of energetic, excited, passionate, future-oriented people and were immediately caught up in it and saw your attitude transformed almost immediately. This is powerful stuff.

Think back to the story of Jairus in the Bible. Jairus' twelve-year-old daughter was sick and dying and Jairus pleads with Jesus to come and heal her. Then someone came from the synagogue and announced that she had already died. Jesus assured Jairus that his daughter would be OK. When they arrived, there was much crying and wailing because Jairus' daughter had already died. When Jesus entered the home he said, "She is not dead, she is merely asleep." The crowd jeered and scoffed at Jesus. What was the next thing that Jesus did before he healed Jairus' daughter? He cleared the room. He didn't want to "work" among all of that negativity. Now if Jesus doesn't want to work around all that negativity, what makes you think that you are strong enough or powerful enough to overcome it!? If you spend too much time around negative people, they will bring you down to their level.

In this third scenario when we test the subject's strength, nothing is said by them or the audience, no suggestions are made, and it is all done silently. All the subjects did was **EXPOSE** themselves to other peoples' thoughts – and it had a dramatic effect on them. Powerful, powerful stuff!

Let's reiterate the first law that affects your behavior:
 ➤ What you *THINK ABOUT* affects you
 ➤ What you *PUT* into your mind affects you
 ➤ What you *ALLOW* into your mind affects you
 ➤ What you *EXPOSE* your mind to affects you

Who Are You Hanging Around?

So it would seem that we should begin to pay much more attention to what we read, what we listen to and who we hang around. What is all of it doing to us? I would be willing to bet that as you read this, you can think of at least one person in your life that you should spend less time around. (Unfortunately, some of you are married to them. Alas we don't have time for that marriage seminar – some other time!) I would also bet that you can think of at least one other person that you should spend more time around – because they lift you up, encourage you and support you in whatever you do. Who are you allowing to be a Wizard to you, and what are they doing to you? Who are you being a Wizard to, and what are you doing to them?

Who are you hanging around? There are two verses in Proverbs that I had always struggled with because they seemed to contradict each other. They are: Proverbs 26:4 "Do not answer a fool according to his folly, or you will be like him yourself." And Proverbs 26:5 "Answer a fool according to his folly, or he will be wise in his own eyes." So which is it? Are we supposed to answer a fool or not? I finally figured it out. Just *stay away* from fools and then you won't have to deal with it!

What do you read? What do you watch? Is it uplifting and positive? If not, consider changing it. If you have a steady diet of CNN and news headlines -- all that is wrong and messed up in the world – you can begin to develop such a fatalistic attitude about the world that you become very negative about everything.

If you don't think that what you watch and listen to affects you – explain advertising to me. Why would a company spend $2.5 million for a 30-second commercial during the Super Bowl if they didn't think it affected you?

What do you watch, what do you see, what do you focus on? It ALL affects you. Have you ever seen that bumper sticker that says, "Stuff Happens"? (They may spell it slightly differently where you live...) Suppose you have that on your vehicle, and you see it every time you get in and out. What do you suppose happens? "Stuff!" Think about this: have you ever seen that bumper sticker on a Mercedes, a BMW, a Jaguar or a Lexus? Probably not. You only see it on beat-up vehicles to which "stuff" happens!

In Mark 4:24 it says, "Take heed what you hear." So whose responsibility is it as to what goes into our minds? This verse is quite clear. It is our responsibility! In fact in 2 Cor 10:4-5 it says "... bring every thought into captivity." It's up to us to decide what it is we think about. We can choose at any moment what we dwell on, meditate on and think about – if it's negative and prevents us from moving ahead in our lives – it's our fault and no one else's. In short we need to think about what we are thinking about.

American developmental psychologist John Flavell in 1979 defined this higher-level thinking (thinking about and taking ownership of what you are thinking about) as ***metacognition***. You will hear many psychologists talking about metacognition today – 2000 years after the Bible had already described its importance!

Worry

Speaking about what you are thinking about... Are you a worrier? What is worry? Worry is merely thinking about, talking about and repeating over and over and over the very things that we don't want to happen. Mathew 6:27 "And who of you by worrying and being anxious can add to your stature or a single hour to your life?" According to Mathew then, worry is pointless. Knowing from Law #1 that what we think about affects us, that what we think about we gravitate toward, it occurs to me that worry is not only useless, but also very damaging and can continually sabotage our better futures. Job put it this way in Job 3:25, "For the thing that I fear comes upon me, and what I dread befalls me." To dwell on and think about those things that we don't want in our lives is almost a guarantee that they will come to pass. It becomes a "self-fulfilling prophecy." ("DON'T DROP THE ARM!")

Contrast that to Philippians 4:8 where it says, "Finally brethren, whatever is true, whatever is honorable, whatever is just, whatever is pure, whatever is lovely, whatever is gracious, if there is any excellence, if there is anything worthy of praise, *THINK ON THESE THINGS.*" Would this verse describe what you spend most of your time thinking about? My guess is it doesn't. Perhaps it's time to change that in your life.

Meditation

There are several references to meditation in the Bible. To meditate is to dwell on, to think about continuously, and to keep our focus upon a particular thing. Consider God's revelation in Joshua 1:8 "This book of the law shall not depart out of thy mouth; but thou shalt meditate therein day and night, that thou mayest observe to do according to all that is written therein: for then thou shalt make thy way prosperous, and then thou shalt have good success."

1 Timothy 4:15 "Meditate upon these things; give thyself wholly to them; that thy profiting may appear to all." What things is he referring to? God's word.

Psalm 1:2 "But his delight is in the law of the LORD; and in his law doth he meditate day and night." What does he meditate on day and night? God's Law.

Psalm 77:12 "I will meditate also on all thy work, and talk of thy doings."

Psalm 104:34 "My meditation of Him shall be sweet: I will be glad in the LORD."

Psalm 119:15 "I will meditate in thy precepts, and have respect unto thy ways."

Psalm 119:99 "I have more understanding than all my teachers: for thy testimonies are my meditation."

Psalm 119:148 "Mine eyes prevent the night watches that I might meditate in thy word."

Psalm 143:5 "I remember the days of old; I meditate on all thy works; I muse on the work of thy hands."

These verses alone should be sufficient justification to stay in God's word. That is where all the good stuff is! Hebrews 4:12 "For the word of God is living and active and sharper than any two-edged sword... dividing the soul and spirit, and discerning the thoughts and intentions of the heart (nonconscious mind)."

Let me ask you one more time: What do you read, what do you watch, who do you hang around and listen to and what is it doing to you? It matters. Don't try to convince yourself that it doesn't. Get a clue -- Even Jesus chose not to "work" around negative people! THINK ABOUT WHAT YOU ARE THINKING about!

INSIGHTS: "What you think, read, say, listen to and who you hang around with you become."

"You are probably the average of the 5 people you spend the most time around."

"The mind is a powerful thing."

"Simply said - Colossians 3:17 ESV 'And whatever you do, in word or deed, do everything in the name of the Lord Jesus giving thanks to God the Father through him.' Dwell only what is good and God centered."

"Taking the example of the arm and steel rod, what can you think/visualize in your area of weakness?"

Chapter 6
YOUR PERCEPTION

We all have bad maps and limiting beliefs. So how did we get all these limiting beliefs, these 'bad maps'? Part of the problem is our perception. Our perception is poor, is inaccurate, is biased and unfortunately is our window to the world. Let me prove it to you. Look at the drawing below.

Do you see an old lady or a young lady?

Old lady or a young lady? It really doesn't matter. The point is that once you have seen one, it's hard to see the other. (Yes, there are both a young and an old lady in the picture!) Psychologists call this a scotoma; I like to call it "lock-on-lock-out". Once we have locked on to an idea, we tend to lock out alternatives to that idea. In other words, once we decide "this is the way the world is"... It is difficult for us to see options, ideas or opportunities that don't look like what we expect to see.

 We all have these kinds of blind spots. **The real trouble with blind spots is that WE CAN'T SEE THEM!** We don't even know they are there or that we are missing anything.

To continue understanding how poor our perception is, in the box below, count the number of times you see the letter "F". After you have counted the "F"s, continue to read.

FINISHED FILES ARE THE RESULT OF YEARS OF SCIENTIFIC STUDY COMBINED WITH THE EXPERIENCE OF MANY YEARS

How many "F"s did you count? Was it less than six? There are six "F"s in the box -- find them! Still having trouble? Count the number of times you see the word "of". Yep, sure enough, there they are!

Is there any doubt in your mind at this point that your perception is poor, is inaccurate and is biased? In fact most of you reading this book would have spent your whole life thinking it is only a 3-F world if I hadn't pointed out the other "F"s to you! Had I not pointed out the other "F"s to you, it never would have occurred to you to even look for more. That's the problem with blind spots. We don't know we miss them and don't know that we should even be looking for them.

If we can create such blind spots with just a few seconds of conditioning, what do you suppose a lifetime of conditioning has done to you? (Especially negative conditioning!)

Think of it this way; if there are six people standing on a street corner and a car accident happens in front of them – how many different versions of the car accident would you hear? Six. Everyone would have a different take on what happened and how it happened. Would you agree that if our perception were 100% accurate, everyone would see exactly the same thing? But that's not the case. So, it should be pretty obvious that everyone's perception varies widely. Some people are conditioned to see opportunity all around them while others never seem to have any opportunities come their way. *"We see things the way we are, not the way they are!"*

In Numbers 13, God instructs Moses to send twelve men into the land of Canaan to scout out the Promised Land. Ten of them came back and reported that it was indeed a land flowing with milk and honey, but it is a land that will devour its inhabitants and is filled with giants that made them feel like grasshoppers. They were fearful and did not want the Israelites to enter the Promised Land. But there were two that didn't see it that way: Joshua and Caleb reported that they could overcome, that the people of the land were merely bread for them to eat and that the Lord would deliver them into the Promised Land. Wow, talk about different perceptions! And yet they all were on the same trip together and saw the same things. The ten were focused on their fears. Joshua and Caleb were focused on the goal and the Lord's promise (who by the way had already done a few minor things for the Israelites, like parting the Red Sea, destroying the Egyptian army, bringing water from the rocks and feeding them for 40 years with manna in the wilderness where there was no food!) *"We see things the way we are, not the way they are!"*

Later on, when we talk about the RAS (Reticular Activating System) you will understand why peoples' perceptions can be so dramatically different.

But while we're on the subject of perception, here's one more for you to try, just to make sure you've been paying attention:

Connect all nine dots in the figure on the opposite page with four straight lines. Once you start don't lift your pencil from the paper.

Give up?

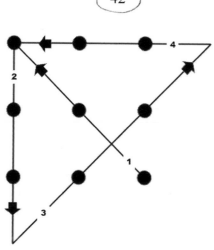

You're probably saying to yourself: "You didn't tell me I could go outside the box!" Who told you that you had to stay inside the box? Most of us have been told our whole lives to stay inside the box, color inside the lines, and do it like everyone else does it. The problem with that is 95% of the time the answers and the opportunities are outside the box. But, we can't see them because we are blind – and what's the problem with a blind spot? – You can't see it and you don't even know that you've missed it or that you should be looking for it. (In Chapter 8 you will understand how the RAS makes you blind)

"We see things the way we are, not the way they are!"

INSIGHTS: "We need to open up our perception."
"We cannot see what we cannot see."

"I need to know what I don't and see what I can't."

"It's easy to notice blind spots in others. What are some blind spots in your life?"

Chapter 7
HOW WE LEARN
WHAT "WE KNOW"

There are two ways that we learn – that we (poorly) perceive the world.

> ➢ **Repetition**

Or

> ➢ **Emotion**

Or both

REPETITION is a very effective way to learn. Repetition is how you got through high school history class. You probably didn't care who did what to whom or when. But you went over and over names and places and dates until you could regurgitate them for the test. That's how I got through Mrs. Binkelman's English class in Senior High School. Let me give you a clue about Mrs. Binkelman – at my ripe old age of 17 it seemed she was about as old as a fossil and the license plate on her car had the birthday of Shakespeare on it – that is definitely a bad sign! One of the things you had to do to get out of her class was to memorize and recite in front of the class the prologue to Canterbury Tales in the old English. I worked for weeks to get it memorized (repetition, repetition, repetition) and 51 years later I still know it. If you repeat something often enough, it goes in deep.

Repetition is why advertising works. You hear it over and over so that when you are standing in front of the grocery store shelf, you gravitate toward the brands you "know."

Growing up, if you hear over and over and over, "You're no good, you'll never amount to anything, you'll be a bum your whole life", you begin to believe it – it becomes your "truth" – it becomes your image of who you are – it's what you "know" about yourself. It then becomes one of your limiting thoughts. (More about limiting thoughts later.)

EMOTION is the second way you learn. Can you remember exactly where you were the first time you saw the image of the second airplane crashing into the World Trade Center? Can you remember where you were when you first saw the explosion of the Challenger Shuttle mission? And if you are old enough, can you remember where you were when you first heard that JFK had been shot? None of these events would ever have to be seen or heard more than once, and you would take them with you to your grave. You will always remember. Why? Because they were so emotional. The more emotional an event in your life is, the more powerful it is, and the faster you learn it and the deeper it goes into your nonconscious mind.

So how do we get to know who we are, what we can do, what we can't do, what our strengths are, what our weaknesses are and what we think we're capable of accomplishing. We can learn it from someone else, like a parent, a sibling, a teacher, a friend, a boss or a stranger. It can be intentional or unintentional; through repetition, through emotion or through both.

MARY AS AN ARTIST

Little Mary is three years old and she just got her first finger-painting set. Mom is well prepared. She puts Mary in her old play clothes. She covers the kitchen table with a plastic tablecloth. She has newspapers covering the floor. Then Mom turns little Mary loose with her new finger paints. Within about five minutes Mary has created the most beautiful finger painting ever. She knows it is an absolute masterpiece. She knows she will be the next Michelangelo. She is so proud and so excited about her new creation.

Just as she is finishing up, her little brother Johnny, seven years old, comes bopping through the kitchen and looks over Mary's shoulder. He says, "Eeeeeeeeew! What is that?!" Mary says excitedly, "It's a cow!" Little Johnny says, "Doesn't look like any cow I've ever seen. Cows have four legs, not three, and by the way the sky is blue not green. Stupidest looking cow I've ever seen!" How does Mary feel at that moment? She's devastated isn't she? One moment she thinks she has created a masterpiece and the next moment little Johnny has straightened her out about that! My guess is that was very EMOTIONAL for Mary, so it goes in deep.

Now, what do you suppose happens whenever Mary looks at that finger-painting set over the next few days? She replays the scene with Johnny over and over – she repeats that painful experience in her mind many, many times. So her first artistic endeavor is very negative, very emotional and is repeated many times in her own mind.

Mary is now five years old and one day she is thinking about how much she loves her daddy. So Mary decides to get out her favorite Cinderella coloring book, take her favorite Cinderella picture and color it for her Daddy as a special gift. She painstakingly stays within the lines. It's the best coloring job she has ever done. She can hardly wait for her daddy to come home from work. She knows that this one is so good that it will end up on the refrigerator door! When she hears him come through the front door, she races to greet him with her picture: "Daddy, daddy, daddy, look what I did for you!" – knowing that it will really make his day. He grabs it out of her hand and says grumpily, "Not bad." As he throws it back at her he says, "I've had a tough day." How does Mary feel right now? She's devastated again. She's thinking to herself, "I guess it really wasn't any good. If it had been, it would have made Daddy happy. But obviously, it wasn't good enough to do that." What happens every time she sees her coloring book over the next few days? She replays that very unhappy scene in her mind over and over and over. She experiences the pain again and again. She reminds herself how bad her Cinderella picture must have been. One more time it hurts when she tried to be creative. It was EMOTIONAL when it first happened and then plenty of REPETITION in her mind whenever she thinks about it, really nails it home.

Mary is now in third grade. It is parents' night at the school. All week Mary has worked painstakingly on her piece of art, because she knows that every child's artwork will be hanging in the classroom for all the parents to see. She knows that this is the best thing she has ever done and can't wait to show Mommy and Daddy. In fact, she knows that it is so good that it is going to end up on the refrigerator door at home! As they enter the classroom and approach the bulletin board where her picture is hanging, Freddie and his parents get there first and his picture is hanging right below hers. There isn't room with all the desks in the way for them all to be there at the same time, so Mary and her parents are waiting as Freddie's parents are looking at his drawing. "Oh Freddie, that is just beautiful! You are so talented. I can't believe you are only in third grade! Most kids in high school couldn't do something that good. Now look at that one above yours. Goodness sakes, in kindergarten you would have been embarrassed to hang that up. That's so sad....... But, Freddie you are amazing and we are so proud of you!"

How does Mary feel right now? She is devastated one more time. It's very painful one more time. Now, she doesn't even want Mommy and Daddy to see her picture and she runs out of the classroom in tears. Mary is a tough kid, but every time she tries to be an artist it hurts and she is finally convinced, "You know, this art thing just isn't for me – I don't need that kind of pain in my life." It's emotional. It goes in deep and it is burned into her nonconscious mind.

So who is it that taught Mary to avoid trying to be creative? It was people that loved her, cared for her and people that would never do anything **intentionally** to hurt her. Think about this: Did anyone ever sit Mary down, look her straight in the eye and tell her, "Mary you have no talent, you are not creative, you will never be an artist, so why don't you just give it up and forget about it?" Of course not. No one would ever dream of saying something like that to a child. But, what happened? Mary MISPERCEIVED the cues, misinterpreted what was going on. All she registered is that whenever she tried to be an artist, *it hurt.*

Quite often, as in Mary's case, it is not the put-downs or negative verbal bruising and battering that many children (and adults) are subjected to; but it is UNAFFIRMED strengths that can cause just as much damage. If we are never affirmed by the important people in our lives for the things we do, we will interpret that to mean that we are bad at them. People that never receive praise as a child spend their lives trying to earn it from those around them and still feel that they can never be 'good enough' no matter what they do.

About twenty-five years go by. Mary has a great job working on the administrative side of a large and successful advertising company. One day Mary's boss walks into the office and says, "Mary, we've been watching you. We are very impressed with your work and we think you have what it takes to go to the top of this company. We want to fast-track you in our management training program." Mary is thinking to herself, "Fantastic! This is what I've been waiting for! My dream is about to be fulfilled!" For the moment she is so excited, that she's about to jump out of her skin. Then her boss goes on to say, "Mary one of the things that we believe in this company, is that for anyone to be successful as a manager, they need to have an intimate understanding of everything that we do around here. So, starting Monday morning, you will be in the art department, doing artwork and helping to lay out some of our advertising campaigns."

What do you suppose flashes through Mary right then? Fear. Is she consciously thinking about those three unfortunate incidents when she was a child? She is not. But nonconsciously fear surfaces. (And nonconsciously is where 90% of our decisions are made.) All she "knows" is that every time she tried to be an artist, it was painful. So out of her mouth comes something that sounds like this: "Frank, I really appreciate that offer and I really do want to go to the top someday. But with two kids at home, I feel like I really need to be spending a lot of quality time with them. You know I'm the kind of person that would give it 100%, and if I were to do that I just wouldn't have enough time for the kids. Thank you so much, but I'm just going to have to take a pass right now."

It sounded really good didn't it? It certainly was sincere. But is that why Mary REALLY turned it down? No, it was more likely that fear surfaced in her and she would do whatever it takes to avoid having to confront that fear – even to sabotaging her career. How often have any of us sabotaged ourselves without quite knowing how or when or even why? Fear surfaces. We're not sure why or where it's from, but we will move in a different direction – or stay the same – in order not to have to deal with the fear. Remember, "We see things the way we are, not the way they are!"

RICK AS A PROFESSIONAL SPEAKER

I am a professional speaker and trainer. I speak nationally and internationally on a wide range of topics. I am comfortable and even relish speaking in front of very large groups and am always seeking opportunities to do so. But it almost didn't turn out that way.

When I was in first grade, during "show and tell" I had brought my brand-new cocker spaniel puppy named "Pokey" to class. You probably think that you had a cute puppy when you were a kid – forget it, mine was cuter! There I was in front of a class of 21 six-year-olds, and you'll never guess what Pokey did. Yep, she did – all down the front of me. It was the funniest thing those first graders had ever seen. They laughed and howled for what seemed like forever. I was mortified, and all I wanted to do was go home and hide.

The next time I can remember being in front of a group was in eighth grade debate class. I thought debate would be pretty easy because I was good at research and memorizing facts and figures. I thought I could beat anyone into submission with enough facts and figures. It's the day of the big debate. I've done my research. I've got all my index cards arranged and organized. I'm prepared. I'm ready for battle. My opponent and I are at the front of the class. My opponent stands up and starts her first presentation and everything is fine. When it's my turn, as I stand up and begin to talk I notice there is sort of a low level tittering going around the class. When I sit down, it stops. The next time I stand up, it starts again, except now it's mixed with laughter. I get more and more uncomfortable to the point that I'm now distracted, not listening to my opponent and finally get so nervous I drop my index cards. I'm embarrassed and totally disoriented as to what is going on because I thought I was doing a good job with the debate, but now all I can think about is that everyone is laughing at me and I have got to sit down and end this. It's finally finished and I totally blew it. (I got a C- when I had been pulling straight A's.) When I got back to my desk, the kid behind me leaned forward and whispered, "Rick, your fly is open!"

The next time I was in front of a group of people was in Mrs. Binkelman's class – Senior English. It was my day to recite the prologue to Canterbury Tales. I had practiced it for weeks. (Repetition, repetition, repetition...) I knew it forwards, backwards and upside down. I knew that I was going to nail it. Her class was right after lunch and I was the first person she called on. I sprang to the front of the room and launched into my recital. I knew I was doing it perfectly and yet the whole class was laughing at me. One more time all I can think about is that I have got to get this finished and sit down as quickly as possible. I fumbled the last few lines and it was finally over. As I sit down, my best friend leans across the aisle and says, "Rick, you've got a big piece of spinach stuck to your front tooth!" Once more I'm embarrassed and mortified, and once more I know that standing in front of a group is a dangerous thing to do if you don't like being laughed at.

Did anyone ever sit me down, look me straight in the eye and tell me that I have no talent, that I can never be a professional speaker? Of course not. Was the laughter because I was doing a poor job of presenting or speaking? No. So how did I learn that it was dangerous to be in front of a group of people? -- Through a mere handful of EMOTIONAL experiences that I MISPERCEIVED and then REPEATED over and over in my mind. And, I ultimately convinced myself to avoid public speaking at all costs.

All of this discussion leads us directly to the SECOND LAW that affects your behavior:

THE SECOND LAW

Your self-image was formed by CLEAR, SPECIFIC, VIVID, EMOTIONAL experiences and/or lots of REPETIION.

One of the reasons I ended up becoming an aerospace engineer was because I didn't think that I would have to interact with other people very much. I had become terminally shy, did everything I could to avoid people and wouldn't even eat lunch in the company cafeteria for fear that someone would sit down next to me and I would have to have a conversation. As long as I was in my little cubicle doing my engineering analysis I was fine. But, the minute I had to ask somebody for information or attend a staff meeting, I was a wreck. I certainly avoided any situation that caused me to have to stand in front of a group.

Ten years go by and I was getting very disgruntled working for the large aerospace corporation and government contractor with all the politics that go with it. I was tired of working for people that I wouldn't have hired. I was actively looking for a business that I could get into on my own. I have always had an entrepreneurial bent and was really tired of working for someone else. We were introduced to an opportunity that looked like it could be my ticket out of corporate America, but very soon I learned that I would have to begin to do presentations to small groups. Fear welled up inside of me and I almost decided right then and there that the business wasn't for me. All I could think about was, "If that's what it takes to be successful – there's no way I'm going to pursue that opportunity!"

But, for the first time in my life I consciously recognized that if my circumstances were ever going to change – I was going to have to change. There's an old adage that says, "If you keep doing what you're doing – you're going to get what you've got." I was going to have to overcome my fear of public speaking if I were going to succeed in the business. Typically, no one will go through major changes unless they have a good enough reason to change. What is a good enough reason to change? A powerful, important and compelling goal. That goal for me was to be independent and not have to work for someone else the rest of my life. That goal was powerful and compelling enough for me to make what seemed at the time to be very scary changes. Was it easy? No. Was it worth it? Absolutely!

It doesn't matter whether it is Mary believing that she isn't an artist or creative, Rick knowing that he can never be a public speaker, or YOU believing that you "can't sell", or "aren't good with numbers", or "not comfortable around strangers", or "will never amount to anything"... We all have some bad maps – some "head trash" that we need to change to keep from continuing to sabotage ourselves and our performance. In fact, perhaps up to 95% of those things we think we can't do we are wrong about. It doesn't matter whether we had a few emotional negative experiences when we were young or we had someone in our lives repeating over and over why we could never measure up – we misperceived the reality, but filed it away as though it were true - and then –proceeded to behave as though it were true. Remember, we see things the way we are, not the way they are.

Perhaps Mark Twain said it best: **"It ain't what you don't know that gets you into trouble. It's what you know for sure that just ain't so."** Most of what you think you're not good at – what you can't do – just ain't so! You're much better than you think you are. "We see things the way we are, not the way they are!"

52

INSIGHTS: "Our self-image is what we have learned not necessarily who we are."

"This is my chapter. Fear has at times consumed me. Sometimes to the point of sabotaging all the gains I have made. Changing my thinking is the first step to overcome my fear."

"ALL life experiences affect your life."

"The past is but prologue."

"It's time to create a different map. What have I been told I cannot

Chapter 8
WHY YOU GET STUCK

HOW BAD DOES IT HAVE TO GET?

Put yourself in this picture: You are in bed by yourself. It's the middle of the night. It is cold. You are cold. In fact, you are so cold that you cannot go back to sleep. Got the picture? The extra blanket is in the closet across the bedroom. How cold do you have to get before you will get up and get the blanket? Be honest now.

Many people would say that they won't get up until they are so cold they have icicles hanging off their nose. Others would say that they need to be "pretty cold." Some would say that they would get up right away and get the blanket. It really doesn't matter what your answer is, because they are all exactly the same answer: the answer is that you won't move until you are "cold enough." Now, "cold enough" may vary from one person to another, but, until you are "cold enough!" there is no way you are going to get up and get the blanket!

Do you know anyone that lives their life that way? Until things get "bad enough" they are not willing to do anything to fix it. When things finally get so bad that they have got to do something, they'll start acting to turn it around. They will continue to do whatever it is until it gets "good enough", and then they will stop doing it until it gets "bad enough." Then they start doing something about it again until it gets "good enough" and as soon as it is "good enough" they quit until it gets "bad enough", until it gets "good enough", until it gets "bad enough", until it gets…

Their whole life pattern is up, down, up, down, up, down, up, down… It never gets much better and it never gets much worse. It's pretty much the same thing day after day after day. What percentage of people would you guess live their lives this way? Right – 95%!

LIFE PLAN 1

I'm glad you've been paying attention. We'll call this pattern Life Plan 1.

Perhaps the most fascinating thing about these people is that I will quite often hear them say something like, "Gee, I wonder what my life will be like in ten years." Well, guess what, it will pretty much be the same as it is today. This isn't rocket science – it ought to be obvious to everyone. (The reason I know this isn't rocket science is because I was a rocket scientist for eighteen years – and this ain't it!)

Wouldn't it be much better if we had life patterns that looked more like Life Plan 2? Sure there are down times, but each down time is higher than the last and each up time is higher than the last, so that there is constant growth, constant progress and a constant progression. Wouldn't that be a much better way to live our lives?

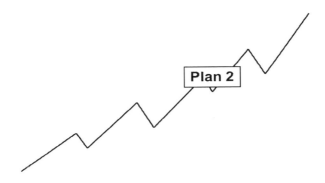

LIFE PLAN 1 OR LIFE PLAN 2?

What is the difference between **Life Plan 1** and **Life Plan 2**? It's really quite simple. In **Life Plan 1** you are at "A"........................ Sure enough, you're at "A" and will continue to be at "A" unless you set some clear, specific, vivid, measurable goals.

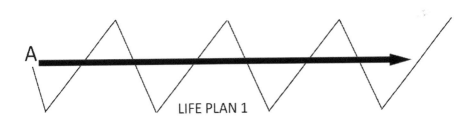

In **Life Plan** 2 you are at "A", AND you are **MOVING TOWARD** "B". So, what is "B"? "B" is a goal. A goal is something that moves you, motivates you, pushes you, pulls you, and drives you – gets you to do something that you wouldn't ordinarily do that is not in your comfort zone.

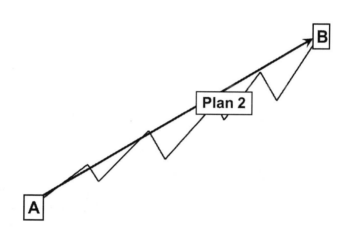

Remember, in Chapter 1 we said that "Without an adequate answer to the question, 'WHY', ANY price is too high to pay"? A goal is your 'WHY'. That is the only thing that can break you out of Life Plan 1. In fact, Proverbs 29:18 says, "Where there is no vision, the people perish." It sounds to me like a goal – a vision of the future - - must be pretty important.

Several years ago my wife and I took our first granddaughter to San Francisco when she was six years old. On one of the days we were there we planned a special trip to Sausalito. We were taking the ferry across the bay by Alcatraz and the Golden Gate Bridge and going to have a very elegant lunch in Scoma's on the pier in Sausalito. We're talking linen tablecloths, real china, real silver and the best fettuccini Alfredo with shrimp you have ever eaten! It was a special event for our granddaughter and had been our goal for several months. When we got up in the morning the anticipation and the excitement level was very high for all of us. It was going to be a great day!

As we were getting dressed I decided to turn on the TV to check out the weather report for the day. I caught the Good Morning America show and the commentator was saying that they had just conducted a survey among Americans. They asked this question: "What do you look forward to the most during the day?" The four most common responses were:

➢ 21% said "Watching TV"
➢ 16% said "Opening the mail"
➢ 11% said "Going to bed"
➢ 4% said "Nothing"

Those were the four most common responses! It looks like at least 52% of Americans don't have much to look forward to! They have nothing to motivate them, nothing to excite them, no reason to take a risk, nothing that will get them to make any changes in their lives. And I'll tell you who the worst ones are; they are the ones that sit in bed, watching TV while they open the mail. Now that's really bad!

The contrast between the responses to that survey and the kind of day we had planned with our granddaughter hit me like a two-by-four. I realized how blessed we were to live life the way we do – to have dreams, to have goals, to be moving toward something of value and especially to realize our goal of making memories for our grandchildren. And in fact that day turned out to be every bit as wonderful as we had planned and anticipated.

The essence of all of that is Law #3 that affects your behavior - - that keeps you stuck in specific life patterns:

THE THIRD LAW

Your performance will never exceed your self-image by very much or for very long.

What is our self-image? It's the compilation we call "the truth" about who we are, what we can and can't do, what our strengths and weaknesses are and what we deserve to have or to accomplish in this world. And where did we get this version of "the truth"? More often than not, we misperceived and misunderstood what was going on around us, but we continue to act as though it is "THE TRUTH".

Remember Mary who was petrified of being an artist? It was her self-image and her fear buried in her nonconscious mind that prevented her from taking that promotion. We see things the way we are, not the way they are.

As you read the Bible, whenever you see the word "heart", if you replace it with the word "nonconscious mind", you will find that 98% of the time you will know exactly what is being said. When you look "heart" up in the concordance, you will discover that in the original Hebrew and Greek it meant "the will", "the intellect", "the inner most being"; sometimes referred to as the "bowels' or the "gut". The word many people use today to describe all of that is "subconscious" – we will call it the nonconscious because I think it is more descriptive. Later on in this book it will become apparent that the reason I am making such a large point of how to interpret the word "heart", is because it is the answer to how we discover the limiting beliefs and "bad maps" that are keeping us from our better futures.

But for now, dwell on this:

Proverbs 27:19 "As water reflects the face, so a man's heart (nonconscious) reflects the man"

Proverbs 23:7 "As a man thinketh in his heart (nonconscious), so is he"

Both of these verses confirm the essence of what Law #3 is saying: You will only perform up to the image you have of yourself. If you have a 'truth' that says, "I don't deserve to be successful, I don't want money because it is bad, I can't do this or that, it hurts whenever I try to …", then guess what – you will continue to sabotage your efforts to make sure that you "stay where you belong."

If fear surfaces in you when confronted with a new opportunity, you will naturally avoid that new situation (a situation that could in fact help you to move ahead). Where do those fears come from? They come from our version of "the truth" (By "the truth" in small letters, I mean "the truth" as we perceive it – and what do we know about our perception? – It stinks. That means that much of what we believe to be "true" probably stinks too! In other words, many of our fears have no basis in fact. You could even think of **F E A R** as an acronym meaning **F**alse **E**vidence **A**ppearing **R**eal) We don't act according to "THE TRUTH" (meaning God's Truth about who we are in Christ and what we are really capable of -- which too often lies dormant in the disillusioned spirit of man). Instead we act according to 'the truth' as we perceive it to be. So if we continue to make decisions about our futures based upon our fears, we will merely continue to recreate "the truth" – to create the very thing that we supposedly would like to get away from.

Psychologists refer to this phenomenon as Cognitive Dissonance. The simple version is that if we behave differently than what we believe, it creates dissonance -- discomfort. It creates discomfort because what we are doing and what we believe don't match. In order to eliminate that discomfort there are only two things that we can do: Either 1) change our version of 'the truth' – OUR CURRENT perceived REALITY or 2) behave in such a way that we will get back "where we belong" to be consistent with our "truth". Most people will choose option 2 – behave consistent with their version of 'the truth' and they end up staying the same.

Think about how many lottery winners have created this very thing. We've all read many stories of people that before winning the lottery they were a $25,000 per year factory worker. All of the sudden they find themselves with several million dollars that they never had before. Three, four, five years later they are a $25,000 per year factory worker. What happened? They only saw themselves as a $25,000 per year factory worker – that's who they are, how they see themselves, and what they think they deserve in life.

Having millions of dollars all of the sudden creates extraordinary dissonance – makes them very uncomfortable. As a consequence they will do whatever it takes to get back "where they belong". They will squander a lot of it on frivolous things, give it away inappropriately, play the stock market and make sure they buy high and sell low, etc., etc., etc. Before you know it, they have proved themselves right. They've lost it all and they're just a $25,000 per year factory worker. *You must become a millionaire inside before you get your million bucks, or you can't keep it!*

Your self-image is much like the thermostat in your home. If you set the temperature at 72 degrees, as your home cools down to about 71 degrees it will turn the furnace on. When the temperature gets to about 73 degrees it turns the furnace off, etc., etc.

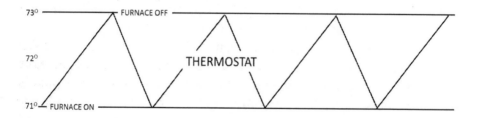

Gee, does that look familiar? The 'performance' of the furnace is controlled by where the thermostat is set. As long as it is set at 72 degrees, the temperature will hover around 72 degrees. The only way we can get the temperature (the performance) to increase is to raise the thermostat. The only way you can get your performance to increase is to raise your thermostat – your self-image.

ARE COMFORT ZONES REALLY COMFORTABLE?

Law #3 describes why we all have "comfort zones". The first thing you need to know about comfort zones is that they are not necessarily comfortable. Do you know someone whose comfort zone is sick? We call them hypochondriacs. Do you know someone whose comfort zone is broke? No matter how much money they earn, they will always spend too much. Do you know anyone whose comfort zone is defeated? No matter how good things are in their life they will find a way to feel miserable about it.

A comfort zone is what you are used to, not necessarily what is 'comfortable'. My Grandmother used to tell me, "Rick, you can get used to hanging if you hang long enough!" That may be a bit extreme, but in effect, it's true.

Suppose you believe that "I'm just not a sales person. I don't like sales people. Selling makes me uncomfortable and I don't like making other people uncomfortable either." One day you find yourself in a job or business that requires that you sell a product or service or even ideas. You are meeting with a client and before you know it they begin to act like they want to buy. But you know that you are not a sales person and you begin to feel uncomfortable. Without even realizing it, you say something or a series of things that talk them out of buying.

You don't really know how you did it, why you did it or even that you did it and you find yourself saying later, "I don't get it. One minute they want to buy and the next minute they don't – what's wrong with these people?" But it isn't the people – it's you. Had they bought, you would have been "selling" – which you know you can't do, and to avoid that kind of dissonance and discomfort you will do whatever you need to do to stay "where you belong" – where you are comfortable – and where you are comfortable is people not buying from you so that you don't have to be a sales person.

If you believe that "I am not worthy of love. I can't ever have a loving, meaningful, fulfilling relationship because I don't deserve it. Every relationship that I have ever had has ended painfully." One day you discover that a new relationship in your life is going well and you might even be coming close to using the "love word" to describe it. You will begin to do subtle little things that begin to sabotage that relationship in order to make sure you get what "you deserve" – in order to stay "where you belong" – in order to prove that "you are right" about relationships in your life.

As you can see there can be some very subtle but pervasive beliefs in our psyche, our nonconscious (our heart) that can continue to cause us to self-sabotage any efforts toward "success" in whatever area of our lives we seem to be stuck. Let me remind you once more of what Mark Twain said: **"It ain't what you don't know that gets you into trouble. It's what you know for sure that just ain't so."** Most of the limitations that *you think* you have are just plain wrong. "The mind that thinks there is a limitation is the limitation."

Learned Helplessness

Another way to look at Law #3 and its effects was defined by the American Psychological Association as what they called the Landmark Theory of the Century. Wow! LANDMARK THEORY OF THE CENTURY. That sounds pretty significant. So what is the Landmark Theory of the Century? They called it "Learned Helplessness".

Much of the research leading up to this theory was done by Dr. Albert Bandura. He wrote a very scholarly book called "Self Efficacy" chock-full of $50 words. It rivals "War and Peace" in its sheer magnitude. Dr. Bandura identified a lot of break-through research in this arena. I will attempt to summarize the essence of it in a few paragraphs (in language that even I can understand).

For purposes of this discussion I would like to make a distinction between self-image and self-efficacy. Self-image encompasses our *feelings* of self-worth. It is our perception of who we are; the compilation of attributes, personality, skills, strengths and weaknesses, etc. Self-efficacy on the other hand is our perception of how much *control* we have over the outcomes in our lives. If you believe that whatever you do really won't make any difference in how your life turns out – you won't do anything to try to change it.

The most important thing to take away from this discussion of Learned Helplessness is that the operative word here is LEARNED. Now if we LEARN helplessness, that also means that we can un-learn, re-learn or learn something new to replace helplessness in our lives. We can learn to be competent, capable and confident. Keep that in mind as I share some of the research and studies that have been done in this area.

An experiment was conducted in which a group of college students (volunteers) were put in a sound booth that had a keypad in front of them with four buttons on it. They were told that they would be subjected to a very loud, strident and discomfiting noise. They were also told that if they could figure out the right sequence of four numbers, it would turn the noise off. As soon as the noise was turned on the students would start trying to figure out the combination, and in a relatively short time they were able to figure it out. After a few successes, it took only a moment for them to put in the proper sequence and turn off the noise.

A second group of students was put in the sound booth and given exactly the same instructions. But, in this case the keypad was disconnected so that no matter what they did, they couldn't turn the sound off. After quite a while and many attempts, they finally gave up and just waited for the experiment to end, enduring the awful noise. After several times of being subjected to this same routine, when the students were put in the sound booth with a <u>functioning</u> keypad, they would just sit there and not even try to turn off the noise even though the solution was right there in front of them. They would sit and endure the noise until the experimenters finally would turn it off. They had learned in a very short period of time to be "helpless". Once you are "helpless" and "know" that nothing you do will make any difference - you quit trying. Once you decide that you have no control over the situation or the future, you just give up.

It is also noteworthy that lack of control can also be incredibly stressful. A fascinating study out of Sweden was done where they looked at the incidence of heart attacks in the work place. The first finding (which should be no surprise to anyone) was that most heart attacks occur on Monday morning. (How many people do you know that hate Monday mornings – having to go to a job they dislike?) But the really fascinating part of the study was that people that **perceived** they had little or no control and no authority in their jobs had a higher incidence of heart attacks than those that **perceived** that they did have control and authority in their jobs. But even more significant was the fact that those people that had had control and authority in the workplace at one point in time, but lost it, had a higher incidence of heart attacks than either of the other two categories of employees. In other words, it is worse to have had control and lost it, than to never have had it in the first place.

There was an experiment conducted in a nursing home where all of the patients were given a gift of a plant for their rooms. Half of the patients were expected to take care of the plants themselves. The other half of the patients had a staff member taking care of their plant for them. The half that had "control" and responsibility for whether or not their plant lived or died lived significantly longer than those patients that had no "control"'. Isn't it interesting that just that little bit of control in their lives could have such a significant impact on life expectancy of the patients?

The common denominator in the behavior and outcomes of all of these studies was the loss of **PERCEIVED** control. People can learn to be helpless; people can learn not to try; people can react in powerful ways to external situations depending upon how they perceive the situation – once they decide that what they do won't affect the outcome.

How do people learn this in the real world that you and I find ourselves in everyday? What about the father that is so overly protective of his daughter, that he won't allow her to do anything on her own for fear she might get "hurt". In fact, no matter what she does, daddy bails her out and she never has to suffer the consequences of her actions. After years of that she goes out into the real world and finds that she is "helpless" on her own expecting someone else to take care of her just like daddy did for so many years.

What about the parent that always explains away a student's bad grades by blaming it on the teacher, or the study environment, or their lab partner? If they can perform at a very low level and always get away with it, they will not have incentive to try harder or work harder on their first job – they are pretty 'helpless'.

What about the boss that punishes new ideas because "that's not the way we've done it around here for the last 20 years!" Pretty soon the employee quits trying to be innovative and improve on the job because they get beat up every time they try.

What about the person that nags their spouse incessantly no matter what they do, how much they do, or how good a job they do? Eventually, they will just quit trying to please the other because no matter what they do, they are going to get nagged anyway, so what's the point in trying?

See how easy it is to learn to be "helpless" and to not try? But remember – it is LEARNED. And much of what we 'learned' we misperceived. (Remember from Chapter 4 how bad our perception really is?) Most of us are much better, more competent, more skilled and more powerful than we think we are. We just misperceived some of the cues that other people were giving us.

The most important thing to take away from the "Landmark Theory of the Century" – Learned Helplessness – is that it was *learned*. If it can be learned, it can be unlearned. Regardless of your view of your own self-efficacy today, you can learn to be more competent, more confident, more effective and more successful in your life. "We see the world the way we are, not the way it is."

INSIGHTS: "WE are who we believe we are."
"You must raise YOURSELF before you raise your GOALS."
"Spend time reflecting on how your life will be in 10 years. If you continue doing what you've always done how will your life affect your finances? Loved ones? Relationship with God?"
"How would you like to see yourself? How would your life be different?"
"If you keep doing what you're doing you're going to get what you've got."

Chapter 9
COMMON MISPERCEPTIONS

There are four areas of limiting beliefs, or "bad maps" that seem to be particularly prevalent among Christians that many people need to deal with before they can begin to see "success" in their lives. Here they are:

1. It is wrong to "want".
2. There is something inherently wrong with money. Poverty and humility go hand-in-hand.
3. Unconditional love and any type of "performance expectation" are incompatible and in conflict with each other.
4. Rewarding someone proportionally to their performance is in conflict with the fact that as Christians we are to treat all people equally.

Obviously, it isn't just Christians that can hold these particular limiting beliefs, but they are very pervasive in the Christian community. I will deal with them one at a time and see if I can convince you how inappropriate they are as well as how limiting they are to our behavior, our potential and as a consequence, our success and our witness.

Misperception #1: "It is wrong to want."

Eskimos have 28 different words for snow. They can describe it in almost infinite variety. Their words describe its characteristics, its structure, its viscosity, their ability to mold or form it, its reaction to a person's weight to describe just a few. Why do they have so many different words to describe snow? Because, it is incredibly important in their lives. They are surrounded by snow. Their very survival depends upon their ability to deal with it.

Skiers usually have about a dozen words to describe snow, and the words may vary somewhat depending upon the part of the country they ski in. In Colorado we have powder, deep powder, champagne powder, packed powder, packed, hard pack, wind pack, crust, breakable crust, corn, slush, crud and mashed potatoes. Back east they also have hard pack, ice, blue ice, slush and crud. Why do skiers have so many words for snow? Because, it's very important to them and will determine their technique, the equipment they use, and whether they even want to go out that day.

All of you non-skiers are sitting there thinking, "Who cares? -- I really don't give a rip!" Why? Because all you care about is that it's that nasty stuff you have to drive around in occasionally and move off of your sidewalk. It's just not that important in the world you live in.

What about a well-educated college graduate on the island of Fiji that has never left the island – how many words for snow do they have? Just one – snow. "Yeah, I heard about that. Rain freezes and turns white. How weird is that?!" It just doesn't matter to them, so they only need one word for snow.

What's the point of all this talk about snow? Simple. Does it make sense that the more important a concept is to you, the more words you will have to describe it? In fact, that is exactly the case.

Try this on for size: There are 25 words in the Old Testament and 15 words in the New Testament that we translate into English with just one word – DESIRE. It occurs to me that the writers of both the Old and New Testaments understood desire much better than we do, and understood its importance much more than we do. When it comes to the concept of DESIRE, we rank right up there with the Fiji islander and the concept of snow. We use only one word to describe something that the Bible writers thought was pretty important and complex. I think most of us just don't get it. Out of curiosity, perhaps we ought to see what the Bible has to say about "wanting" – about DESIRE. See if there any patterns that you pick up on as you read the following verses. Dwell on each of them a few moments.

Proverbs 13:12 "Hope deferred makes the heart sick, but when desire cometh it is a tree of life."

Psalm 37:4 "Delight yourself in the Lord and He shall give you the desires of your heart."

Proverbs 11:23 "The desire of the righteous ends only in good."

Proverbs 10:24 "The desire of the righteous will be granted."

Proverbs 13:19 "A desire fulfilled is sweet to the soul."

Proverbs 21:25 "The sluggard's desires will be the death of him because his hands refuse to work."

Proverbs 15:6 "The house of the righteous contains great treasure, but the income of the wicked brings trouble."

2 Thessalonians 3:10 "If any would not work, neither shall he eat."

Proverbs 10:4 "Lazy hands make a man poor, but diligent hands bring wealth."

Proverbs 24:33 "A little sleep, a little slumber, a little folding of the hands to rest, and poverty will come on you like a bandit and scarcity like an armed man."

It sounds like DESIRE is a pretty desirable thing doesn't it? So, is DESIRE good or bad? Desire is neither good nor bad – it is neutral. It is not about whether DESIRE is good or bad. However, there are some qualifications that precede DESIRE for it to be OK. Reread the above scriptures. It comes down to whether or not you are walking in God's will and whether or not you are willing to work.

It should be pretty obvious that if **_you are walking in God's will_**, He will give you the desires of your heart (knowing that your heart is right with God.). But He also requires that **_you work_**. Yes,

God is perfectly capable of just dumping it in your lap, and yes, He will do that on occasion. But there are too many Christians that spend an inordinate amount of time praying for God to bless them, but aren't willing to do anything themselves to improve their lives. Walking in God's will and willingness to work – if you have those two things going for you, DESIRE is OK.

Can you see that if you have a belief that it's not OK to "want", it's not OK to DESIRE, you will behave in such a way to ensure that you don't get anything? Our performance will never exceed our self-image by very much or for very long. (Law #2)

Misperception #2: "There is something inherently wrong with money. Poverty and humility go hand-in-hand."

It might be instructive, before we get into this one, to have a feel for what you think about money and rich people. Take a piece of paper and divide it into three sections. In the first section, describe what it is like not to have enough. How does it affect your relationships? How does it affect decisions that you make? How does it make you feel about yourself?

In the second section, write down the comments you heard the most as a child when the subject of money or rich people was brought up in your home. Is there any correlation between these "beliefs" and how you relate to money today?

Here are the ones I heard the most growing up:

"Money doesn't grow on trees you know."
"We'll always be broke."
"Rich people stepped on somebody to get it."
"Poor people are more righteous than rich people."
"Humility and poverty go hand-in-hand."
"Money is the root of all evil."
"We can't afford it."

How many of those sound familiar?

In the third section of your piece of paper, write down what it would be like to have abundance, to have more than enough, to have great gobs of money? How would that make you feel? How would it affect your relationships? What different decisions would you make in your life? Think about this: How many of your "bad maps" that you learned about money as a child have kept you from the abundance you deserve?

Many Christians I know, including myself, were taught either explicitly or implicitly from the pulpit that poor people were somehow more righteous than rich people and that it is much better to be poor than rich. Well, we better back up the truck on that one. Try this verse out:

Proverbs 22:4 "Humility and the fear of the Lord bring riches, honor and life."

When you look "riches" up in the original Hebrew, it is referring to worldly wealth. Most people interpret that verse to mean "spiritual wealth", but that is not at all what it says. From this verse, it doesn't look to me like humility and poverty go hand-in-hand. It looks to me like humility goes hand-in-hand with riches, honor and life.

There was a period in my life that I had a real burden for poor people. Because of my sympathy (not empathy) for them, I thought I should become like them. It didn't help. I found that I could do much more good for poor people by having money and resources, than not having them. Check these verses out:

John 10:10: "I have come that you might have life and have it more abundantly." [Abundance in the original Greek is referring to worldly wealth.]

Proverbs 10:22 "The blessing of the Lord maketh rich and he adds no sorrow to it."
[Again, "rich" means worldly wealth.]

Proverbs 1:32 "The prosperity of fools shall destroy them."
[A fool in the original Hebrew was someone that has turned their back on God.]

Proverbs 10:16 "The wages of the righteous bring them life, but the income of the wicked brings them trouble."

Proverbs 13:21 "Misfortune pursues the sinner, but prosperity is the reward of the righteous."
Deuteronomy 8:18 "Thou shalt remember the Lord thy God, for it is He that giveth thee the power to get wealth."

Psalm 1:1-3 "Blessed is the man who does not walk in the counsel of the wicked or stand in the way of sinners or sit in the seat of mockers. But his delight is in the law of the Lord, and on His law he meditates day and night. He is like a tree planted by springs of living water, which yields its fruit in season and whose leaf does not wither. Whatever he does prospers."

3 John 2: "Beloved, I wish above all things that thou mayest prosper and be in good health, even as thy soul prospers."

What have you been hearing from all of these verses? Is money good or bad? Money is neither good nor bad – money is neutral. It is your relationship to money that is the issue. If you are walking in God's will and you are good stewards, money is not a problem. But if you turn your back on God and are controlled by avarice and greed, money is a huge problem.

Invariably however, there will be people who try to beat you up with:
Matthew 19:24
Mark 10:25
Luke 18:25
Where it says: "It is easier for a camel to go through the eye of a needle than for a rich man to enter the kingdom of God." So what are

you going to do with that one? Gotcha now! How about we read the next two verses: "The disciples were amazed and asked, 'Who then can be saved?' Jesus replied, "With man it is impossible, but not with God. With God all things are possible." Jesus didn't say that a rich man couldn't get into heaven. All He was saying is that you had better be walking with God.

Did you ever hear this preached from the pulpit?

"Money answereth all things." **(Eccl 10:19)**

Yep, it really does say that. That must be why money is one of the most addressed subjects in the Bible. If you still have some negative feelings about money, it's time to get over them. Money is not the issue. It is only your relationship to money that is the issue. Yet, it could be your negative attitudes about money that have kept you from achieving what you have wanted or needed in that arena.

There are many Christians that are fearful that money will change them. But, money doesn't change you – it only makes you more of what you already are. If you're a drunkard – you have more to drink. If you're a giver – you have more to give. There are others who believe that rich people are controlled by money. I think quite the opposite is often true. It is people without enough money that are controlled by it, because virtually every decision they make is based upon whether or not they can afford it – not whether it's the right thing for them in their lives.

There are many of you reading this book that would say, "I'm comfortable. I don't need much. Why should I work to get more money?" Look at it this way. If you have a good marriage, but you could make it better, should you? Of course. If you have a strong walk with the Lord, but you can make it stronger, should you? Absolutely! Are you ready for the zinger? If you are making enough money, but you can make more, should you? YES! And give it away! There are millions of people in this world that will never have your skills, your abilities or your opportunities and they need you to be as successful as you can, so that you can help them. If you are at a place in your life where you are "comfortable", my goal before you finish this book is to make you uncomfortable!

There are some caveats however.

1 Tim 6:17 "Command those who are rich in this present world not to be arrogant or put their hope in wealth, which is so uncertain, but to put their hope in God who is the one who provides us with everything for our enjoyment."

And, it is also important to realize that with wealth, comes responsibility.

Luke 12:48 "To whom much is given, much is expected."

Misperception #3: "Unconditional love and any type of 'performance expectation' are incompatible and in conflict with each other."

Many Christians seem to have a real problem with being evaluated for their performance – that somehow it devalues them as people if they do not live up to other people's expectations. Their attitude is that, "If you really loved me unconditionally, as we are supposed to as Christians, you would value me even if I don't perform up to your expectations." There is an inherent flaw in that logic. None of us as Christians doubts that God loves us – and yet God has expectations that we will perform in His kingdom (The Lord's Prayer: …. On earth as it is in Heaven). We can love someone unconditionally and still have expectations of them.

One thing that I have noticed over the years is that people who are performing love accountability, and people who are not performing hate accountability. And those that aren't performing will use the "unconditional love" argument to justify to themselves and others their lack of performance. But like it or not – all of us need accountability! The following verses will help put accountability into perspective.

Hebrews 6:8 "But land that produces thorns and thistles is worthless and is in danger of being cursed. In the end it will be burned."

Revelations 20:12 "And I saw the dead, great and small, standing before the throne, and books were opened. Another book was opened, which is the book of life. The dead were judged according to what they had done (on earth) as recorded in the books."

1 Peter 4:5 "But they will have to give account to Him who is ready to judge the living and the dead."

Revelations 20:13 "The sea gave up the dead that were in it, and death and Hades gave up the dead that were in them, and each person was judged according to what he had done." [On earth]

1 Peter 4:6 "For this is the reason the gospel was preached even to those who are now dead, so that they might be judged according to men in regard to the body, but live according to God in regard to the spirit."

There are hundreds of references throughout the Bible about judgment. Judgment implies that there are certain expectations related to our "performance". There is no doubt that we will be judged based upon what we accomplish in THIS world prior to our homecoming in heaven, and yet, God still loves us unconditionally.

Misperception #4 - Rewarding someone proportionately to their performance is in conflict with the fact that we are to treat all people equally.

REWARDS are the next issue that Christians seem to have a challenge with. Not only should people be rewarded for performance, but should the rewards be proportionate to the performance? (As opposed to the idea that we all should be rewarded equally because of God's unconditional love.) Let's see what God says about the subject:

Jeremiah 32:19 "Great are your purposes and mighty are your deeds. Your eyes are open to all the ways of men; you reward everyone according to his conduct and as his deeds deserve."

Psalms 62:12 "….and that you, oh Lord, are loving. Surely you will reward each person according to what he has done."

Psalms 18:20 "The Lord has dealt with me according to my righteousness; according to the cleanness of my hands has he rewarded me."

Matthew 16:27 "For the Son of Man is going to come in His Father's glory with His angels, and then He will reward each person according to what he has done."

Jeremiah 17:10 "I the Lord search the heart and examine the mind, to reward a man according to his conduct, according to what his deeds deserve."

Proverbs 14:14 "The faithless will be fully repaid for their ways, and the good man rewarded for his."

Revelations 22:12 "Behold, I am coming soon! My reward is with me, and I will give to everyone according to what he has done."

Matthew 5:19 "Anyone who breaks one of the least of these commandments and teaches others to do the same will be called least in the kingdom of heaven, but whoever practices and teaches these commands will be called great in the kingdom of heaven."

Proverbs 13:21 "Misfortune pursues the sinner, but prosperity is the reward of the righteous."

Hebrews 11:6 "And without faith it is impossible to please God, because anyone who comes to Him must believe that He exists and that He rewards those who earnestly seek Him."

So where are we? In the Lord's Prayer, Jesus says, "…. Thy kingdom come, thy will be done, on earth as it is in heaven." Truth is parallel. In other words, heaven is a model for us to emulate here on earth. God not only rewards, but He rewards proportionate to our deeds, our accomplishments and our behavior. Why would we think that it is any different here on earth? Why would we think that a different set of rules applies in this world? We know that God loves us unconditionally, but our rewards will be proportionate to our performance.

Summary

Let's look at all four of these misperceptions together. As long as we are walking in God's will and willing to work, "wanting" and desire are OK. Money is a tool and a means to an end; in many cases, the vehicle to achieve our wants and desires – whether it is to have more freedom to pursue our passion, to support the kingdom financially, to provide for our families, or anything else that God has put in our hearts. Money in and of itself is not a bad thing. It is how we relate to money that is at issue. There is an expectation that we will perform up to our potential in every area of our lives and that we will in fact be rewarded according to our performance. Perhaps the following verses will help put it all together for you:

Ecclesiastes 3:13 "That everyone may eat and drink and find satisfaction in his toil – that is the gift of God."

Proverbs 12:24 "Diligent hands will rule, but lazy hands end in slave labor."

Proverbs 13:4 "The sluggard craves and gets nothing; but the desires of the diligent are fully satisfied."

Proverbs 13:21 "Misfortune pursues the sinner, but prosperity is the reward of the righteous."

1 Corinthians 3:8 "The man who plants and the man who waters have one purpose, and each will be rewarded according to his own labor."

We need to expect people to perform and to reward them accordingly. If they don't live up to their potential, should I still love them unconditionally – of course! Do I have to reward them for their lack of performance – No! And we need to be able to recognize that rewards and unconditional love are distinct and separate. In reality, love is much more than that and much different than that:

"Love is patient, love is kind. It does not envy, does not boast, and is not proud. It is not rude, it is not self-seeking, it is not easily angered, it keeps no record of wrongs. Love does not delight in evil, but rejoices in the truth. It always protects, always trusts, always hopes, always perseveres. Love never fails." (1Corinthians 13:4-8)

Unfortunately, the world thinks that to love is to reward. But 1 Corinthians 13 doesn't say a thing about rewards. A gift or reward can be an expression of love, but it is not love – just as a reward for a certain behavior, or performance is not love.

PRIDE COMETH BEFORE THE …

Recognition is a way of rewarding people for their performance. Many Christians think that recognition causes people to fall into the sin of pride – it's OK to be successful as long as you don't "feel" successful. I know parents who have refused to ever compliment their kids on a job well done because they are afraid the kids will get "a big head". It usually creates the exact opposite of what we want. Kids that are never affirmed go through life constantly seeking affirmation and recognition, feeling that they can never be "good enough". As adults, that can lead to an individual that is focused solely on achieving from a worldly perspective, seeking constant recognition and losing sight of their relationship to God. We have to allow people to enjoy their successes. Consider what the apostle Paul said:

Philippians 3:14 "I press on toward the goal to win the prize for which God has called me heavenward in Jesus Christ."

2 Timothy 4:8 "Now, there is in store for me the crown of righteousness, which the Lord, the righteous judge, will award me on that day – and not only to me, but also to all who have longed for his appearing."

1 Corinthians 9:24-25 "Do you not know that in a race all the runners run, but only one gets the prize? Run in such a way as to get the prize. Everyone who competes in the games goes into strict training. They do it to get a crown that will not last; but we do it to get a crown that will last forever."

2 Timothy 2:5 "Similarly, if anyone competes as an athlete, he does not receive the victor's crown unless he competes according to the rules."

The implication from Paul seems to be: "I am determined to succeed! I will win! I feel good about what I will have accomplished!" Well, if all truth is parallel, then there is no reason to believe that these principles don't operate in the secular world. So where is the problem with recognition? There is no problem if we recognize that God is the source of our successes; if we stay focused on Him and give Him credit for what we achieve in life. If we fail to recognize that all we have accomplished through our GOD-GIVEN skills and abilities has its power and source through our creator, then pride rears its ugly head.

How often have you heard an athlete say after a victory, "I give God all the glory!" or "I thank Jesus Christ for blessing me!"? Would you rather they say in a mousy morose tone of voice, "It was really nothing. I just got lucky. Any other day it could have been someone else." It occurs to me the first response has a much higher probability of attracting someone new into the Kingdom, or building the faith of a believer.

A successful Christian who is willing to declare to the world that "It is God that accomplished this in me", is a tremendous witness. To assume that a Christian that is successful is less righteous than one who is not, is wrong. Success and righteousness do not oppose each other. But what we do need to remember is that our righteousness does not come through our works or our success. Righteousness comes through our walk with the Lord. Is it more difficult for a "successful" Christian to maintain their proper perspective with God? – Yes. Does a "successful" Christian that is visible in his community carry more responsibility as to what he does and how he operates in this world? – Yes. But, it is possible to be both successful (through our own efforts and God's blessing and provision) and righteous (through Christ) as long as we remember:

Deuteronomy 8:18 "But remember the Lord your God, for it is He who gives you the ability to get wealth, and so confirms His covenant, which He swore to your forefathers as it is today."

And

1 Timothy 6:17 "Command those who are rich in this present world not to be arrogant or put their hope in wealth, which is so uncertain, but to put their hope in God who is the one who provides us with everything for our enjoyment."

And

Luke 12:48 "To whom much is given, much is expected."

In conclusion then:

Proverbs 16:3 "Commit to the Lord whatever you do, and your plans will succeed."

Matthew 6:33 "Seek ye first the kingdom of God and His righteousness and all these things will be added unto you."

The bottom line is this: If we correct our misperceptions and align ourselves with what God's word really says, we can experience God's best, help others and advance the Kingdom.

INSIGHTS: "All things come from God."
"Praise be to God for giving us all we need for direction in your word!"
"It is the love of money, not money itself that is evil."
Discipline: Always be aware that my nonconscious (heart) feelings will probably be wrong and preserver seeking God's will and direction for my life and business.
Tool: Prayer and staying in God's word.

Chapter 10
YOUR R.A.S.

It's time for the last piece of the puzzle – the "how come I don't do what I'm capable of doing to be successful?" puzzle. The answer is that the Reticular Activating System is in cahoots with your nonconscious mind (your "heart").

At the base of your brain, where all the nerve endings come together to form your spinal cord, there is something about the size of your thumb called the Reticular Formation. This is a real physical, physiological thing. Part of the Reticular Formation is the Reticular Activating System (RAS). The RAS has one job and one job only. Its job is to filter information; and it is superb at what it does. We are constantly exposed to, and bombarded by so much information, data, stimuli and even opportunities, that if we consciously tried to register it all, process it all and think about it all, we would literally go crazy. We would be in a constant state of "overload". So the RAS (which remember, is VERY good at what it does) constantly filters out "extraneous" and "superfluous" information and data. It's like a "Spam Filter" for your mind.

The crucial question then becomes: How does the RAS determine what it needs to filter out? The RAS is constantly asking three questions in order to decide "what you need to know and be aware of":

1. "Is it my responsibility?"
2. "Is it important?"
3. "Does it match my version of 'the truth'?"

Whatever information, data or stimuli you are exposed to must satisfy all three questions. It's not the best two out of three. It is not a democracy or majority rules. It must satisfy ALL THREE criteria before the RAS will allow you to be aware of it. Let's look at each one of these three filters so we can begin to understand why your perception is so poor, why you have blind spots and why you can't see opportunities that are all around you.

---

1. "Is it my responsibility?" – This is the
first question the RAS is constantly asking.

Have you ever gone someplace you've never been before, in an unfamiliar part of town, as a passenger in someone else's car? After you got there did you realize that you had absolutely no idea how to find your way home? It has probably happened to most of us. On the other hand, had you driven there yourself, would you have been able to find your way home? More than likely. Why in the first case were you clueless, but in the second case you noticed the gas station on the corner, the white picket fence, the church steeple and all the other landmarks that would help you find your way out of there? Because, in the second case you knew you were responsible for getting there and back. However, in the first case you knew you weren't responsible, so your RAS decided you didn't need that information, filtered it out and you never saw the important landmarks that could help you find your way home.

MOM...

I would like all of you mothers reading this book to think back to when your first child was an infant (I'm sure the following was true of all of your children, but think especially of your first child). They were just old enough that they had graduated from the bassinet by your bed to their own crib, in their own room down the hall. The first few weeks do you remember how you would be sound asleep in the middle of the night, and out of a sound sleep, all of a sudden you knew that you had to be down the hall checking on your child? You don't know what you heard; you're not even sure that you had heard anything; you just knew you had to be there, and in a heartbeat you are wide awake and at that child's bedside making sure that everything is OK.

It's the third time this particular night that you have been up to check on your child. As you return to your bed, you decide that it is important for your husband to know that THIS! - IS! - THE! - THIRD! - TIME! That you have been up to check on HIS! child. So, you THROW! yourself on the bed and JERK! the covers back over to you, just to make sure your husband appreciates that this is the THIRD! time you have been up to take care of HIS! child – and your husband sleeps through the whole thing. He never heard you get up, was never aware that you came back to bed, and never even felt you jerk the covers back over.

Now, in some of your homes, later that night, the family dog starts yapping in the back yard. Dad jumps out of bed, throws open the window, shouts at the dog to shut up, comes back to bed – and Mom sleeps through the whole thing. How is it that Mom can hear a virtually inaudible sleeping baby, but can't hear barking dogs and Dad can hear dogs, but can't hear babies? It's simple – in your home the roles have been defined such that Mom is responsible for the baby and Dad is responsible for the dog. Your RAS will filter out any information that you are not responsible for and make you unaware of it.

I've often heard it said that wisdom comes with age. But, that is not true. The only thing that automatically comes with age – is old. That's all you get. Wisdom comes when you accept responsibility for your life. I know 80-year-olds with no wisdom and 18-year-olds with plenty. The difference is that the 18-year-old has accepted responsibility for their life and future, but the 80-year-old is still blaming everyone and everything around them for their stature in life.

All of us spend about the first nine months of our lives on a waterbed. It is warm. It is cozy. All of our needs were met without us having to do a thing. Then we are born, the doctor cuts the umbilical cord, slaps us on the rear end and then 95% of us spend the next 50 years of our lives looking around for someone else we can plug our umbilical cord into to take care of us. But, it's not someone else's responsibility. And <u>until you take responsibility for your life and future, your RAS will make you blind to opportunities around you.</u>

---

2. "Is it important?" – This is the second question the RAS is constantly asking.

Right now, I would like you to stop feeling your shoes. (If you don't have any shoes on it doesn't count!) But, if you do have shoes on right now, you can't stop feeling them – you are very aware of them. Before you read this paragraph, you were probably not aware of your shoes at all, but as long as you continue to try not to think about them, you are very aware of them. Why? Because all of the sudden I "made it important" by talking about it and as long as we continue to talk about your shoes, you will continue to be very aware of them. However, before I brought it up, you were totally unaware of your shoes. The RAS knew that those stimuli were not important and thus, filtered out the information so that your conscious mind would not have to deal with it. And, a few minutes from now, after we have stopped talking about your shoes, your RAS will again filter out that information because it knows it isn't important and you will once again be unaware of your shoes.

Think about where you are sitting right now. Can you hear a refrigerator motor running, the hum of fluorescent lights, the fan from the heating or air-conditioning system, traffic outside, city noises or any other background noise that is common in your home? Until I just now asked you to stop and focus on it, it was unimportant and your RAS filtered it out. The vast majority of the time you never consciously hear or pay attention to any of those types of noises, because they are "not important".

For those of you that read a daily, big-city newspaper, can you tell me how many stores had ads for dishwashers on sale in Friday or Saturday's paper? I'm sure you have no idea whether anybody was even advertising dishwashers at all. But let's suppose you walk into your kitchen today and find two inches of water because your dishwasher has blown up – how many ads for dishwashers on sale will you see now? EVERY ONE. They will jump off the pages at you. Why? Because all of the sudden it is important information to you. (By the way, Sears has had at least one model of dishwasher on sale every weekend for the last 40 years!)

A few years ago our niece and her husband bought a beautiful, expensive home high on Point Loma in San Diego. From their back deck there was a magnificent view of the Pacific Ocean, San Diego Bay and downtown San Diego. Interestingly enough, however, it sat right in the take-off pattern of the San Diego airport. When a 747 would take off with all the burners cooking, it would rattle the windows, dishes in the china cabinet would dance on the shelves and there was no way that you could continue a conversation until the plane had passed over head and the roar had ended.

Aldona and I went to visit them about a year after they had moved into this home. I'm a pilot. I've spent a lot of time around airports. I love airplanes. There is nothing about planes or flying that scares me. We walked in their front door for the first time (not knowing that there was an airport out their back door!) and as we stood in the living room, a 747 took off. It sounded like it was going to come right through the house. I literally ducked! As I ducked, I said, "Whoa – what was that?!!!!" For a moment my nephew had this blank look, like 'what the heck is wrong with you?' And then with perfect equanimity, not understanding why I reacted the way I did, he said, "A 747." I noticed during the three days that we were there, that whenever a plane took off, the family would stop in mid-sentence, pause until the plane passed over, and then pick up the conversation as though nothing unusual had happened. They had been there long enough that they no longer heard, registered or reacted to 747's flying over the house. Why? Because the RAS knew it wasn't important information – so they literally were deaf to the noise. By about the third day I wasn't paying any attention to 747s either.

That's the same reason that people that live next to railroads or highways never 'hear' what would drive someone else crazy (until they too had lived next to it long enough). Once your RAS knows that the stimuli, the information is not important, it filters it out so that you don't have to "deal with it."

For future reference, there is a huge clue here. If the information, data, stimuli or **opportunities** that you are exposed to must satisfy the question "Is it important?" how do we let our RAS know what is important to us? To be continued in Chapter 12 ...

---

3. "Does it match my version of the truth?" –
This is the third question the RAS is constantly asking.

Let me remind you that your version of "the truth" is what you think about yourself – your self-image – what you think you deserve or don't deserve, your strengths, your weaknesses, your skills or lack thereof, who you think you are and what you think you are capable of, and what you can have and do in this life. All of this is filed away in your nonconscious mind (your heart).

So let's start with:

Proverbs 23:7, "As a man thinketh in his heart (nonconscious mind), so is he."

This is where cognitive dissonance comes into play one more time. To maintain your sanity, you must behave consistently with what you believe. The easiest way to do that is for you to perceive things the way you believe they are. How often have you said about someone else (not that YOU would ever be like this!), "Oh, he only hears what he wants to hear."? It's true. The RAS will typically only allow those things into your conscious mind that are consistent with what you believe to be true. If it doesn't match your version of "the truth", it will filter it out – you will quite often not even be aware of information, data or circumstances that are not consistent with what you believe. We are literally blind to what is around us.

You see, if we are bombarded with too much information that is different than what we believe, one of three things has to happen:
1. We will go crazy

2. We must block the info, or

3. We have to change our belief system.

If we really do want to change our lives, which option do you think would be the best? It should be pretty obvious that we need to change our belief system – especially since we know that we have a lot of limiting beliefs and "bad maps"! Which option do you think most people choose most of the time? #2 – block the information so that we don't have to "deal with it".

Think back to the earlier example of selling. If you don't think you are a "salesperson" or you have negative feelings about selling, your RAS will make you unaware of any buying signals the prospect may be giving you and only allow you to register anything that you could construe as an objection. They may merely be asking a simple question for clarification, but you will perceive it as something negative, indicating (falsely to you) that they don't want to buy. If they get too close to buying, you will even say things that will turn them off so that they don't follow through with the purchase – even if they really wanted to. You do this totally on the nonconscious level. You never intentionally and consciously shoot yourself in the foot, but all the same you sabotage the interaction just so you can be sure to prove one more time that you really are not a "salesperson". Law #3 comes through again: Our performance will never exceed our self-image by very much or for very long.

In summary, the RAS will only allow you to perceive accurately those things that satisfy **ALL THREE** criteria: 1. "It is my responsibility!" 2. "It is important!" 3. "It does match my version of the truth!"

You may be exposed to an opportunity that could be very important to you and even matches your version of "the truth", but if you haven't taken responsibility for your future, your RAS will make you blind to it. You may have taken responsibility for your future and you may be exposed to an opportunity that even matches your version of "the truth", but if your RAS doesn't know that it is important, your RAS will filter it out.

If we really do want to move ahead in our lives, then the crux of the problem becomes -- How do we let the RAS know what is important and how do we change our version of "the truth"? Now that we have identified how and why we get stuck, how we continue to sabotage ourselves and why we stay in unproductive patterns, we will figure out in the rest of this book how to fix it.

These types of self-defeating patterns repeat themselves over and over, so we continue to get what we have always had (Life Plan 1). The only way we can break out of these patterns is to do three things:

1. Take ownership (responsibility) of our lives and futures
2. Have a powerful and compelling goal that gives us a reason to change; a goal that is clear, specific, vivid and measurable (**so the RAS knows exactly what is important to us**)
3. Raise our self-image – our version of 'the truth' -- of who we are and what we deserve to have in life so that we can perform UP TO our real God-given potential. (Law #2)

Remember, "We see things the way we are, not the way they are!"

WILL YOU FIX IT?

Perhaps the most important question you could ask yourself right now is, if you come across a deficiency, if you discover a blind spot or if you find some "bad maps", are you willing to fix them? Think about it before you respond. Remember the "Three Good Questions"? The second one asked, "Are you willing to do whatever it takes to be successful?" The real answer for most people is "no".

I've observed over the years that when confronted with a deficiency, people with high self-esteem will fix it; people with low self-esteem will blame others for their problems. We know from our discussion of the RAS that people that blame others and don't take responsibility for their lives will always be blind to the very things that could help them move ahead.

People with high self-efficacy (a la Albert Bandura...), those who perceive they have control over events in their lives are more likely to act to improve their situation, to take a risk, to get out of their comfort zone, to challenge themselves and to change and grow.

Carol Dweck in her book *"Mindset"* describes it another way. (I highly recommend this book!) She says that people often have either a "FIXED Mindset" or a "GROWTH Mindset". Here is how she describes the difference:

MINDSET	**"FIXED"** MINDSET Leads to a desire **to look smart** and therefore a tendency to:	**"GROWTH"** MINDSET Leads to a desire **to learn** and therefore a tendency to:
CHALLENGES	…avoid challenges	…embrace challenges
OBSTACLES	…get defensive or give up easily	…persist in the face of setbacks
EFFORT	…see additional effort as fruitless or worse	…see effort as the path to mastery
CRITICISM	…ignore useful feedback	…learn from criticism
SUCCESS OF OTHERS	…feel threatened	…find lessons and inspiration
THE RESULT	They may plateau early and achieve less than their full potential	They reach ever higher levels of achievement

The bottom line is that if you are predominantly a "Fixed" mindset, you are *less likely to fix things* that are holding you back even if you recognize that your self-image is sabotaging you, because then you would have to admit that you were wrong.

But perhaps more importantly, even if you are predominantly a "Fixed Mindset" – know that you can change it, you can grow, you can become more growth oriented. You are not stuck there if you don't want to be.

INSIGHTS: "It is important to know how to change our RAS."

"Looks like I have a 'Fixed Mindset'! Good to know that my actions are the result of a scientific reason and thank God that it can be fixed. The question is...do I have the courage?"

"We must be willing to change our mindset if we want to succeed."

Chapter 11
GOD'S GIFT OF IMAGINATION

When you finish reading this paragraph, close your eyes and put yourself in this picture: You are standing on the roof of a 30-story building. You are very aware of the fact that there is no wall, no guardrail, nothing to prevent you from falling. With your eyes closed, imagine yourself walking to the edge of the building, planting your toes right on the edge, and looking straight down 30 stories. (Now close your eyes…)

How did that feel? Many people find they can't force themselves to even imagine doing such a thing. If you actually did it you probably experienced some fear and trepidation and had a very real physiological response – you may have broken out in a sweat, you may have felt the hair on the back of your neck stand up, you may have felt the muscles in your neck and shoulders cramp up or any other type of response that would have been typical if you had really walked to the edge of a 30-story building.

Have you ever been in a serious car accident or a had a very serious close call, that whenever you thought about it days or even months later, you could once again feel a surge of adrenaline go through you? Just thinking about it and imagining the consequences makes you "feel" exactly what you felt when it first happened. You get the same physiological response, and yet you are perfectly safe as you sit and think about it.

I was a technical rock climber when I was younger and had some rather harrowing experiences and close calls. I have a fear of heights, but as long as I trusted the person on the other end of the rope to belay me safely, I was usually able to overcome that fear. But when

I think about some of those close calls, even today, I can feel that surge of adrenaline.

I was climbing Mt. Princeton (14,000+ feet) in February. We were trapped by a blizzard and a whiteout just below the summit at about 13,700 feet and had to spend the night up there. The temperature was at least 40-below. The reason I know that is because that's the lowest my thermometer registered, and the mercury just curled up in the ball at the bottom and refused to come out! We had on every piece of clothing we had brought with us as well as our expedition-weight down parkas. With all our clothing and parkas on we were in our down expedition sleeping bags and still just lay there and shivered all night. Most of my toes got frostbite that night. I have never been so cold before or since. Forty years later, whenever I think of that night I still shiver.

How often have you heard a particular piece of music and were immediately transported to an event that was very significant in your life – complete with all the sights, sounds and emotions that occurred the first time? Have you ever smelled a certain smell, and were immediately back in Grandma's kitchen, with all the emotions that were attached to that experience?

The point of all this is the basis for:

THE FOURTH LAW

Your nonconscious mind does not know the difference between a real event and a vividly imagined one.

Why is that important?
Finish this sentence: "Practice makes _____."

But is that really true? In fact, PRACTICE *MAKES PERMANENT*. What if you practice the same bad habits over and over? You get perfect bad habits. What if you replay your failures over and over in your mind? You make those failure-oriented behaviors permanent. It's time to begin using your imagination to your benefit and God's intent instead of to your detriment. Stop replaying your failures over and over in your mind.

Denver has a severe case of "Bronco Mania." You can hardly turn on the TV without some kind of coverage or commentary about football – even during the off season. I've often found it interesting how after a loss, when they interview the coach and the players, they say, "We need to go back to the game tapes and see what we did wrong." They are repeating their mistakes over and over in their minds – and making them permanent. Shouldn't they be reviewing what they did right instead?

The way that Law #4 can work to your benefit is this: "Perfect practice makes perfect". And where is the one place you can have perfect practice every time? **YOUR IMAGINATION!** Do you realize that you are the only "animal" in the animal kingdom that has an imagination? Only you can envision the future. Your imagination is a precious gift from God to be used appropriately in your life. It is a powerful tool and you can use it in such a way that it works to your advantage – or to your disadvantage. Your mind is an incredibly powerful thing. But, always remember who the power source is – God.

Don't find yourself in the situation like the Methodist, the Baptist and the positive thinker, all of whom found themselves in hell one day. They were sitting around discussing how they ended up there. The Methodist said, "I don't get it. I don't know if I missed that particular Sunday or if the preacher wasn't very clear, but I really don't understand why I'm here." The Baptist said, "Oh, I know exactly how I got here. They were really clear in my church! There's no doubt in my mind." All the while the positive thinker is sitting on a rock going, "It's not hot, and I'm not here. It's not hot and I'm not here. It's not hot and ...." Your mind is powerful, but it's not that powerful!

I am convinced that one of the reasons God gave us this extraordinary gift that we call imagination is so that we can intentionally create CLEAR, SPECIFIC, VIVID experiences the way that we would like them to be. We can begin to envision the future the way we would like it to become. We can begin to see our lives the way we would like them to turn out. We can start to see ourselves behaving in such a way that we can create the life of our dreams.

Remember, "Without a vision the people perish." And what is a vision? It is our ability to see the future differently than the circumstances we currently find ourselves in.

What does all this mean in terms of beginning to make the changes in our lives that will allow us to move ahead? Do you recall what Law #2 said? "Your self-image was formed by clear, specific, vivid (emotional) experiences and/or lots of repetition." So, if that's the way your self-image was formed, *what is the only way that your self-image can be changed?* – Through clear, specific, vivid (emotional) experiences and/or repetition, *WHETHER REAL OR IMAGINED (Law #4),* because your nonconscious mind (your heart) does not know the difference between a real event and a vividly imagined one. So there you have the Fifth Law.

THE FIFTH LAW

Your self-image can be changed by clear, specific, vivid, emotional experiences and/or repetition, whether real or <u>imagined</u>.

Your imagination, "practicing your future perfectly", thinking positively about your future are all necessary to begin the change that you want in your life – but they are not sufficient. They are not ALL that you need. The changes you want have to take place in the real world with its challenges, problems, obstacles and disappointments.

We will come back to this in Chapter 14 when we "rethink positive thinking". But for the moment we need to address the ongoing conversation you have with yourself.

INSIGHTS: "Nonconscious does not know what is real or imagined."

"Starting to realize the mindset and strongholds that have truly kept me captive for 40 years. The thoughts of 'You can't do anything', 'You'll never succeed', 'Other people can do all that, not you' echo in my head. Every time I have tried I have done well but not for long. I always failed."

"You can 'imagine' yourself to a better life."

"Let your imagination flow. Spend time painting the picture of your better future."

Chapter 12
THE SECRET TO DISCOVERING
YOUR LIMITING BELIEFS

If you have gotten this far in the book I am going to assume that you really do want to change, that you do want to grow, that you would really like to know and understand what the limiting beliefs and 'bad maps' are that have kept you from achieving all that you know you are capable of achieving. You are about to find out what is buried down there in your nonconscious mind (your heart) that has been sabotaging your performance. Are you ready? Are you sure? Do you really want to know what is stopping you? OK, here goes...............
If you don't really want to know, this would be a good time to quit reading and close the book. This is your last chance...

OK. Here is where you find the answer:

Matthew 12:34 "For out of the abundance of the heart (the nonconscious) the _mouth speaketh_"!!

This is huge. Read it again. Read it about ten times, just to make sure you got it. Read it again. Read it tomorrow and the day after. Read it next week, next month, and next year!

In other words, whatever there is the most of in your heart (your nonconscious mind), will overflow into your words, your language, your conversation. All you have to do to figure out what is stopping you is to listen to your words. Not just the words you speak out loud, but also the running conversation you have with yourself.

Pay particular attention to how you talk to yourself when you make a mistake or mess it up. That is probably the truest reflection of how you think about yourself. There is a very high probability that it is your words, your internal dialogue you have with yourself, that is preventing you from changing and moving ahead in your life because you are continuing to affirm being the kind of person that you don't want to be.

"I DON'T TALK TO MYSELF....."

Everybody talks to themselves continually. You have an on-going conversation about everything that is happening around you. Of course some of you right now are saying to yourselves: "Is that true? Do I really talk to myself? I don't think I talk to myself. No, I don't talk to myself. Only crazy people talk to themselves. Ooooops – I guess I do talk to myself......"

Since this is a continual part of your waking life, do you suppose that the words that you say, the conversation you have with yourself affects you in any way? Or is it just irrelevant gobbledygook? I would like to propose that this is one of the most significant areas of your life that probably needs fixing.

Does this sound at all like you when you mess it up? "I knew it. I always mess it up. I never get anything right. I don't know who I'm trying to kid – I'll never be successful. I've never been successful up until now. Why in the world did I think it would be any different this time? I've never done anything of significance. Everyone I know thinks I'll never amount to anything. They're right. It's never going to change. Who am I trying to kid. I am such a joke. It's pointless to keep trying."

Or if someone doesn't return your phone call, are you saying to yourself, "They obviously don't want to talk to me. In fact, they're probably mad at me and don't even like me anymore. I'm evidently not important enough for them to take a couple of lousy minutes out of their schedule to pick up the phone. Everything and everyone is always more important than me. I'm such a loser that I can't even get my supposed friends to call me back."

Sounds pretty toxic doesn't it? Remember, one of the ways we learn is through repetition. Our continually negative self-talk is constant repetition and reaffirmation of the very things that we DON'T want in or lives. It is virtually impossible for us to change if we don't change our self-talk. Our words are dramatically more important than most anyone thinks. Try a few of these on for size:

Proverbs 6:2 "Thou art snared with the words of your mouth."
[I've heard it phrased, "Hung by the tongue!"]

Ephesians 4:29 "Do not let any unwholesome talk come out of your mouths, but only what is helpful for building others up according to their needs, that it may benefit those who listen." [Would that describe what comes out of your mouth most of the time?]

Matthew 12:36-37 "On the day of judgment men will have to give account for every idle word they speak. *For **by your words** you will be justified and acquitted, and **by your words** you shall be condemned and sentenced.*" [He didn't say you would be either condemned and sentenced or justified and acquitted by your actions and deeds, but BY YOUR WORDS. Perhaps we do need to pay a bit more attention to what we say and speak.]

Proverbs 18:21 "Death and life are in the power of the tongue."
[That's a pretty scary thought given what comes out of most peoples' mouths most of the time.]

Proverbs 12:14 "From the **fruit of his lips** [your words] a man is filled with good things as surely as the work of his hands rewards him." [What is just as important as your effort? **Your words!**]

Ecclesiastes 10:12 "The words of a wise man's mouth are gracious; but the lips of a fool will swallow up himself." Enough said.

Mark 11:23 "For verily I say unto you, that whosoever shall say unto this mountain, be thou removed and be thou cast into the sea; and shall not doubt in his heart, but shall <u>believe</u> that those things which he saith shall come to pass; he shall have whatsoever he <u>saith</u>." [The two operative words here are <u>believe and say.</u>]

Matthew 15:11 "It is not what enters into the mouth that defiles the man, but what proceeds out of the mouth, this defiles the man."

Proverbs 21:23 "Whoso kept his mouth and his tongue keepeth his soul from troubles."

1Peter 3:10 "For he that will love life, and see good days, let him refrain his tongue from evil, and his lips that they speak no guile."

Wow! Is there any doubt in your mind now, that what you say is important? Your nonconscious mind (your heart) merely believes what you tell it the most (repetition, repetition, repetition). In Chapter 13 we will be talking about doing af**FORM**ations as a way to raise our self-image. But a few af**FORM**ations a day in the face of sixteen hours of negative self-talk don't have a prayer of having the effect that you want.

SQUIRREL-PROOF BIRD FEEDERS

So now we have to address the whole issue of squirrel-proof bird feeders. First of all, I'm not sure there really is such a thing. I've bought several over the years. (I actually believed what it said on the box in the hardware store!) It may have taken a week. It may have taken a month. It may have even taken the whole season. But eventually, I always found squirrels in the bird feeders. You see, after I put the feeder up, all those squirrels thought about non-stop was how to get into my feeder. Twenty-four hours a day. Seven days a week. It never occurred to them that they couldn't get into the feeder.

Who do you think stands the biggest chance of success? – Some 'genius' that spends a mere few hours designing the bird feeder, thinking that he can outsmart a squirrel – or a squirrel that thinks of nothing but how to get into the bird feeder until he is in the bird feeder.

Whatever you think the most about, you will gravitate toward. Continual negative self-talk will defeat you, but positive self-talk will dramatically increase your chances of success.

It occurs to me that our self-talk should reflect what God says about us instead of all the toxic words that seem to come out of us all too often. Here are a few verses worth remembering:

I am fearfully and wonderfully made. (Psalms 139:14)

I am being renewed daily. (2 Corinthians 4:16)

I am the righteousness of God. (2 Corinthians 5:21)

I am created to be the reflection of His glory. (Ephesians 1:12)

I am exalted to the right hand of God the Father Almighty, a joint heir to the kingdom of God with Jesus Christ. (Romans 8:17)

I am forgiven. (Colossians 1:13-14)

I am a new creature. (2 Corinthians 5:17)

I am led by the spirit of God. (Romans 8:14)

I am strong in the Lord and in the power of His might. (Ephesians 6:10)

I am above only and not beneath. (Deuteronomy 28:13)

I am more than a conqueror. (Romans 8:37)

I am an overcomer by the blood of the Lamb and the word of my testimony. (Revelations 12:11)

I am able to do all things through Christ who strengthens me. (Philippians 4:13)

I am casting all my cares upon Jesus. (1 Peter 5:7)

I am blessed coming in and going out. (Deuteronomy 28:6)

I am an overcomer. (1 John 5:4)

I am blessed. (Ephesians 1:3)

I am called by God. (Romans 8:28)

I am provided for all things by God. (Philippians 4:19)

It sure doesn't sound to me like any Christian should have a struggle with low self-esteem and negative self-talk, assuming they really do believe what God says in His Word.

Your words are incredibly important. Until you fix your internal dialogue as well as your external conversation, you cannot expect to change yourself! Start monitoring your self-talk. Pay particular attention to what you sound like when things do not go well, because that is the truest indicator of how you see yourself. Remember Law #2. We learn through emotion or REPETITION. Our internal dialogue is a constant REPETITION of what we believe, what we think we can have or do, what we think we deserve and what we think we are capable of. Until we quit repeating all the negative stuff to ourselves, we are fighting a losing battle. We will return to this later because it is one of the keys to accomplishing true change in our lives.

INSIGHTS: "What we speak to ourselves is important."

"Wow, the beginning of this chapter really affirms my insight from Chapter 12. Since you didn't read my mind, I guess a lot of people experience the same thing. Time to move forward and correct it. I never realized that I talk to myself but it's true our minds are always working, problem solving and analyzing everything. I need to do all that to God's glory too. Not going to be easy but the hard work will be life changing!"

"What do you spend the most time thinking about?   What do you think God would have you think about?   How should your self talk sound?"

Chapter 13
IT'S TIME TO CHANGE

To this point we have talked about five of the six laws that affect your behavior as well as several other important concepts about how we got to be who we are, where we are, why we tend to get stuck and why change is difficult. It is time to put all of these concepts together and figure out how to begin the process of change, to become the person God wants us to become. We each need to use all of the God-given potential that we have to accomplish significant things in our lives. Law #6 will set the stage for that change:

THE SIXTH LAW

When you raise your self-image, your performance will increase

---

When you raise your self-image your performance HAS TO increase because you will always behave in a way that is consistent with your beliefs. Cognitive dissonance can actually work in your favor!

Here are the concepts we now need to tie together:

➤ How our thinking affects our performance

➤ How to alter our perception of the world to see opportunity around us

➤ How to get the RAS to allow us to see those things that will help us grow

➤ How to raise our self-image

➤ How to change our self-talk to be supportive of our goals

➤ How to use our imagination to our advantage

➤ **Finally, how to make it all work in the real world of responsibilities, relationships, the press of our commitments and the everyday stresses of life while achieving a balance between our spiritual walk and the real world.**

WHY NOT, WHY NOT YOU, WHY NOT NOW?

There is an old proverb that says, "The best time to plant an oak tree was 50 years ago. The next best time is today."

I know sometimes it feels like we are beyond hope. That we are too old. That we've been this way too long. That it is too late to change. But the answers are much simpler than you might expect. The only challenge is: Do you want to change bad enough to form the disciplines in your life that will allow you to make those changes? Yes, it will take work. Yes, there will be disappointments. Yes, you will fall back occasionally. But every new discipline will affect every other discipline. For every new discipline sown, you will harvest a multiple reward. If you are willing to put in the time and the effort, you can change. You can learn some simple skills and disciplines that will allow you to start moving toward those dreams and goals that you may have given up on years ago. Is it worth it? You bet. Can you 'teach an old dog new tricks'? Yes. Is it too late to start now in your life? No. Will you be glad you did? I'm sure of it. So let's get to work.

INSIGHTS: "Raise your self-image and your performance will improve."

"What I realize is that things that hold me back and are negative affect more than just me. It is like a rock thrown into still water. The rings that form around the site of entry extend as far as there is water! My change in attitude and self-esteem has affected family, friends, and co-workers. The changes I make will also spill out and hopefully help others at least think about it."

"It's never too late to change."

"Are you ready to change? Spend time describing how change would feel. What your life will be like if you do."

Chapter 14
THE BEGINNING OF
YOUR NEW BEGINNING

It should be very apparent by now that until we change our thinking, nothing much will change in our lives. We must change our thinking at the same time we begin to change our self-talk, our behavior and our activities or we will eventually revert to our old behaviors no matter how much self-discipline we muster up. Here are some verses that express very well how crucial this change in thinking is:

Ephesians 4:22-24 "….that you rid yourself of the old nature with your previous habits ….. that you be renewed in the spirit of your mind, and that you put on the new nature that is in God's likeness in genuine righteousness and holiness."

2 Corinthians 4:16 "…. Our inner nature is being renewed every day."

Romans 12:2 "And be not conformed to this world [the 95%], but be transformed by the renewing of your mind that you may prove what is the will of God [in your life]."

Colossians 3:2 "Set your minds on things above, not things of the earth"

All of this is very doable for the Christian. Perhaps the most important verse for you to dwell on is 1 Corinthians 2:16, "But <u>we have the mind of Christ</u> and do hold the thoughts and purposes of *His* heart." **Believe THAT! If you believe nothing else.**

OPENING UP THE RAS

The first place we'll start our transformation is by learning how to get the RAS to open up and allow us to see the opportunities that are all around us all the time. Let me remind you that the RAS is continuously asking three questions that must ALL be answered in the affirmative before you will become aware of opportunities:

1) Is it my responsibility?
2) Is it important?
3) Does it match my version of 'the truth'?

RAS: Question #1
Is it my responsibility?

Number one should be pretty obvious by now. We must consciously and intentionally take responsibility for our lives and our futures. It is time to stop fussing about whom or what "did it to us". No more blaming our parents, our siblings, our teachers or our bosses or any other "dysfunctional" aspect of our lives. If we assume that someone else or everyone else is to blame for who and where we are, then it must be up to someone else to fix us – and they are a little too busy with their own lives to be worrying about ours! Today we take ownership of our lives. From this point in time on, we must decide that what happens in our lives is up to God and US.

RAS: Question #2
Is it important?

The only way that the RAS will know what is important is if **we tell it** **EXACTLY** what is important. We do that by having CLEAR, SPECIFIC, VIVID AND MEASURABLE goals. Let me ask you to do a brief exercise to begin defining your goals. On a sheet of paper, take a few moments to write down 50 things that you would like **to do, to have, to see, to become or to accomplish** over the next 10 years. (Big or little – get them all down.) Don't continue reading until you have done it. If you continue to read without doing the exercise you will miss the impact of the exercise and what we will be talking about next.

Here are a handful of examples:
➢ Take my parents to Hawaii for their 50th anniversary
➢ Start a Bible study in my home
➢ Buy my daughter new volleyball shoes
➢ Save $150,000 for my sons college fund
➢ New granite countertops in the kitchen
➢ Spend at least 2 hours a week reading without guilt
➢ Have Sunday brunch with the family after church every week
➢ Fresh flowers on the dining room table every week
➢ Give $500 per month to missions
➢ Take Dad fishing 3 times per year
➢ Furnish granddaughter's dorm room in college
➢ Get a new lawnmower
➢ Etc., etc., etc.

Go on. Get out that sheet of paper and start writing. Don't skip ahead. Stop reading now and do it! Ah, ah, ah – I caught you. Don't go to the next page yet -- DO THE EXERCISE NOW.

OK. Now wasn't that interesting? You may have found the exercise to be a real struggle. You may have found it difficult to get to 50 things (if you got there at all) and it took much longer than you would have expected. Your self-talk may have even sounded like this: "Hmmmmmmm. Fifty things. That's an interesting question. I've never really thought about it before. I wonder .... Well, gosh I really don't know. Maybe .... Uuuuuh ... Well, maybe a new house. Yeah, that might be kind of nice. Oh get serious. You know that'll never happen. Well, uh, at least maybe, uuuuh, well a trip to Hawaii would be nice. Boy, that'll cost a lot. Oh what the heck, I might as well write it down – I've got to get something on this stupid piece of paper. What else could I write down? I guess I'm pretty comfortable. I really don't need that much to change in my life........ This is really a pretty silly exercise anyway."

How sad would that internal conversation – that self-talk be? And yet, it is all too common. When I ask people to do this in a live seminar, typically two-thirds of the participants can't even come up with 25 things that are important to them and about one quarter struggle to even get 15 things on the page in the length of time it takes a couple of focused people to write down 50. As I watch people's facial expressions during this exercise, I can see the frustration they are experiencing. By this point in the day they know the importance of having CLEAR, SPECIFIC, VIVID, MEASURABLE goals and yet they come to realize they really don't have many or any.

YOUR 100TH BIRTHDAY INTERVIEW

One way that you can begin to gel in your mind the things that really matter to you is to write your hundredth-birthday interview. Suppose you are being interviewed on your 100th birthday. What would you like people to know about you? What lessons would you share? What would you like to have accomplished by then? How would you like to be known? What significant things have you done with your life? How have you affected those people you care about? How have you contributed to the world around you? What have you done to advance the kingdom of God? Answering these kinds of questions will begin to help sharpen your focus about what really matters in your life.

Make no mistake. Setting goals is one of the most crucial things you can do to create a better or different future than you are currently headed for. Remember: "If you keep doing what you're doing you will get what you've got." Now that would be a serious bummer wouldn't it?

Jeremiah 29:11 "For I know the thoughts that I think toward you, says the Lord, thoughts of peace and not of evil, to give you a future and a hope."

Imagine that. God thinks about our future! He declares that we should have hope. He declares that we should have a confident expectation of blessing and provision. God also speaks of doing new things:

Isaiah 42:9 "Behold, the former things have come to pass, and new things I declare; before they spring forth I tell you of them."

Isaiah 43:18-19 "Do not remember the former things, nor consider the things of old. Behold, I do a new thing, now it shall spring forth; shall you not know it?"

Proverbs 16:9 "A man's heart plans his way, but the Lord directs his steps."

Proverbs 3:5-6 "Trust in the Lord with all your heart and do not rely on your own understanding. Acknowledge Him in all you do and He shall direct your paths."

A thoughtful look at these scriptures shows us that God is not intending to do something capricious, impulsive or erratic with our lives. Not only does He have new things in store for us, but He wants us to know about them. Just one more justification to stay in His word so that we can discern His will for our lives. When we do that, we can rest assured that our goals will line up with His goals for us and He will direct and bless our endeavors.

DO YOU KNOW WHAT YOU REALLY WANT?

In my live seminars I always ask participants, "How many of you have gotten to this point in your life and no one has ever asked you what is important to you, much less have asked you to write down those things that are important to you?" Typically one-third to one-half of the audience will raise their hands – regardless of whether they are in their 20's or their 80's. How sad is that?

You have got to ask yourself, how can anyone go through life and never think about and write down what they care about? In fact, my experience has been that about 95% of the population (ever see that number before?) will spend more time planning a one-week vacation than they will spend planning their lives. No wonder they are stuck. No wonder they are on Life Plan 1. No wonder things never seem to get much better.

Telling the RAS what is important begins with knowing what it is you want. Let's begin to refine that list of 50 things that you wrote down (hopefully you came up with 50 things by now). Next to each item that you wrote down put either the letter S, F, P, B or C. The letters stand for: Spiritual, Family, Personal, Business/Financial or Community. In other words, identify each item on your list as to whether it is a Spiritual goal, a Family goal, a Personal goal, a Business/financial goal or a Community (charitable/volunteer) goal. I'm sure some of them will overlap a bit, but put the letter that is the most predominant for that particular goal. OK. Stop reading now and go do it! Really, go do it. Really, do it now!
Caught ya! OK, which part of go do it do you not understand?

Now that you have identified each item on your list of 50, go back and add up how many fall into each category – how many S's, how many F's, how many P's, how many B's and how many C's were there? How did you do with BALANCE? Before you respond to that question, think about this: If you are in full-time ministry wouldn't you naturally have more 'spiritual' goals than someone that is not? If you are married with four kids, wouldn't you naturally have more family goals than someone who is single? Balance is not about having equal numbers in each category. Balance is about having the appropriate number in each category based upon your values. No one else should ever presume to tell you what that balance should be in your life, except God!

But, based upon YOUR VALUES would you say that your goals are relatively well balanced? If not, it is time to start putting some thought into where the emphasis in your life should be, or you will forever be dissatisfied with where you end up.

HOW MUCH, HOW SOON?

The next thing to do with your list of 50 is to go back through and put a 1, 3 or 10 next to each item. Is it a one-year goal, a three-year goal or a ten-year goal? After you have finished identifying each item, add up how many 1's, 3's and 10's you have. How did you do with balance?

If you discover that you have lots of 1's and very few 3's or 10's, you belong to the school of thought that says, "I want it all, and I want it right now!" If that describes you, you need to burn this phrase into your brain:

"I can have anything I want, but I can't have everything I want."

Why not? Because there isn't enough time to <u>do it all right now</u>. You have got to assess some priorities and decide what the most important things are for you in your life and get focused on them. If you attempt too much at once, at best you will do a mediocre job at all of them, and at worst you will fail miserably at most of them.

One of my favorite movie lines of all time was in *City Slickers* with Billy Crystal and the late Jack Palance. Jack Palance was the surly old cowboy, Curly. Billy Crystal was the city slicker, Mitch. They rubbed each other the wrong way throughout the movie but in this particular scene they had left the rest of the gang to roundup stray cattle. Curly abruptly reins in his horse and says to Mitch:

Curly: "Do you know what the secret of life is?"

Mitch: "No, what?"

Curly: "One thing." (Holding up his index finger)

Mitch: "Your finger?"

Curly: "One thing. Just one thing. You stick to that and everything else don't mean s**t."

Mitch: "That's great, but what's the one thing?"

Curly: "That's what you've got to figure out."

THAT IS WHAT <u>YOU</u> HAVE GOT TO FIGURE OUT!

What is your "one thing"? What is important enough in your life that it is worth getting out of your comfort zone, taking a risk, doing something different and forming new disciplines so that you can grow into the person that God intended you to be?

WHAT WILL GET YOU GOING?

In identifying your 1, 3 and 10-year goals, if you found that you have very few 1's, but mostly 3's and 10's, you have a different challenge. If all of your goals are way out in the future, your nonconscious mind figures that you have all the time in the world to get them done, so there is no urgency to start now. We all need some near-term goals to get us moving now and some mid-range and long-term goals to keep us excited about our futures.

WHAT WILL KEEP YOU GOING?

Think about a nine-year-old one week before Christmas. How would you describe her? She is probably excited, with high anticipation, motivated to be on her best behavior so she doesn't get the proverbial lump of coal in her stocking and she is going the extra mile for Mom and Dad. Describe a nine-year-old two hours after all the presents are open. "Is that all there is? Mommy I'm bored. Isn't there something to do around here?" What created the initial excitement and enthusiasm? Was it the goal, or the anticipation of the goal? You have to agree that it is the anticipation, not the actual achievement of the goal that created the change in attitude and behavior. It is fairly apparent that we need near-term goals to create the immediate motivation, activity and behaviors necessary to change our circumstances, but we also need goals that are farther out so that we don't become bored or complacent when we have achieved our more immediate goals. That is why balance here is so important.

GET SPECIFIC

If we want to set goals that really affect our behavior and cause us to change, they must be CLEAR, SPECIFIC, VIVID and **MEASURABLE**. Remember THE FIFTH LAW:

THE FIFTH LAW

Your self-image can be changed by clear, specific, vivid, emotional experiences and/or repetition, whether real or <u>imagined.</u>

For our RAS to open up to opportunities around us, we must tell our nonconscious minds EXACTLY what it is we want, because the

<u>RAS WILL SETTLE FOR ANYTHING THAT WORKS!</u>

That means that if your goals are vague, general, or fuzzy the RAS will shut down the minute anything satisfies what you have told it.

For example, suppose your goal is that you want "more money". You could find a $5 bill lying on the ground and your RAS says, "All right! You met that goal, so you don't need to see any more opportunities in the money arena." You see, the $5 bill is "more money" than you had before. On the other hand, if you had specified exactly (**measurable!**) how much more money you wanted (say, $2500 per month), then your RAS doesn't shut out opportunities until you have reached that specific amount that you want.

What if your goal is "to spend more quality time with my kids"? Any extra time you spend would satisfy that goal so that just an additional two minutes a day would be enough for you to quit looking for and seeing opportunities to spend time with your kids. Better that you set your goal as "I will spend a minimum of 20 minutes each day, with each of my children, engaged in conversation one-on-one with no TV, Game Boy, cell phone, texting, email or other distractions in the room" (clear, specific, vivid, MEASURABLE!).

Suppose your goal is "to be closer to the Lord." Not only does your nonconscious mind (your heart) not know what that means, but it wouldn't know if you had actually accomplished it. As a consequence your RAS has no idea what you need to be aware of to satisfy it. But, "I will spend a minimum of 20 minutes every morning before leaving for work, in prayer, reading at least one Bible chapter per day and lifting up the prayer needs of my family. I will make a point of attending church three out of four Sundays, and read at least one inspirational book or listen to one inspirational CD (or Mp3) every month."

Now you have a way of knowing whether or not you are 'successful' and if you are even moving in the right direction, because you now have a way to measure your progress. This will open up your RAS and begin to alter your behavior in order to achieve it. (Clear, specific, vivid, and MEASURABLE!) Please understand – ANYTHING can be MEASURED, and until you get specific, your behavior and your awareness will not change.

Try this one: "I want to lose weight." Remember what we said in Chapter 3 about your nonconscious mind only responding to the positive attribute of a statement (don't think about a pink elephant!)? It is important that our goals describe what we want and not what we are trying to get away from. If your goal is "I want to lose weight", then your nonconscious mind is focused on the weight you are trying to lose instead of the weight you would like to be. Your goal should sound more like, "I am at my ideal weight at 135 pounds." This has the same effect that "steel rods, power and strength" has during a strength test as opposed to "Don't drop your arm, don't drop your arm, don't drop your arm."

My father was a superb woodcarver his whole life. As a child I was always fascinated to watch him and had made some rather feeble and futile attempts at carving myself. One evening when we were camping my dad was sitting by the campfire carving a dog from a piece of wood he had picked up along the trail during the day. After watching this dog emerge from the piece of wood and thinking about the frustrations I had had at carving, I asked him, "Dad, how the heck do you do that!?" My Dad thought for a moment and then said, "Well Rick, it's really quite simple. All you have to do is take away everything that doesn't look like a dog." At the time I thought that was about the stupidest thing that I had ever heard. But, it was profound enough that I never forgot it, until such time as I finally understood it. What my dad was saying was that I needed to have a vision of what I wanted, not what I didn't want. All I could see was the piece of wood. All my dad could see was the dog.

Have you got a vision for your future? Do you know what you want it to look like? It's not a good idea to be like the person that says, "I always wanted to grow up to be somebody. I guess I should have been more specific." Let me emphasize - *If you don't know where you are going, you are already there!*

"Where Are All The Presents?"

Having clear, specific, vivid, measurable goals helps us know what it is we are to be focused on, how to assess our priorities and allows us to proceed more directly to where we want to end up.

I'm often reminded of our oldest granddaughter, Kristina, when I think about the power of goals and how they affect our behavior. For about 25 years we lived in the mountains west of Denver, in South Turkey Creek Canyon. Every year we cut our own Christmas tree from the mountain behind the house. (And for all you tree-huggers out there, yes, I planted five for every one that I cut!)

The tradition was that I would go out on the first Saturday in December to cut the tree. When Kristina was four and one half years old, she wanted to go with me to cut the tree. She had been so excited that she had been talking about it for weeks. The big day came. There was about a foot of snow on the ground, which wasn't much to me, but to a 4-½ year old, that was knee deep. So, we got her bundled up in her snowsuit, mittens, hat and boots and she was rarin' to go. It was quite a climb to the meadow at the top of the mountain where we would cut the tree – about 700 feet elevation gain – but Kristina insisted on doing the climb herself, even though I offered to carry her. She was really proud of herself when we got to the top – and rightfully so.

We came to the edge of the meadow, and on the other side I spotted a beautiful Colorado blue spruce that was about 20 feet tall. (We had an 18-foot cathedral ceiling in the living room.) As I pointed it out, I said to Kristina, "Look, there's our Christmas tree!" Her eyes got real big with a big smile on her face. But it lasted only a moment. She began to squint at the tree across the meadow, got a big frown on her face and looked up at me and said, "Where are all the presents?!" Talk about a goal-oriented child! It was all I could do to keep from bursting out in laughter at her rather limited understanding of the world. But I was delighted to see how focused and goal-oriented she was! That's what got her to the top of the mountain all by herself – thinking the presents would already be under the tree.

To brighten her back up, I suggested we play a game. I said, "Kristina, let's see who can make the straightest tracks in the snow to the tree." She thought that was a great idea. So, she took one look at

the tree and then lowered her eyes and concentrated very carefully on putting one foot in front of the other – one foot in front of the other – one foot in front of the other...... After about 50 steps she looked up and discovered she wasn't even headed toward the tree and when she looked behind her, her tracks had wandered all over the meadow. On the other hand, my tracks were dead straight toward the tree.

What was the difference? I had kept my focus on the tree. Kristina had been focused on where she was – her circumstances. Sound familiar? Too often people stay focused on where they are instead of where they want to be. It is important that we stay focused on our goals, and not on our circumstances. When we do we are more likely to get to the goal. So again, what is your "one thing"?

Where Is The Horizon?

If you were standing high up on the bridge of a cruise ship, you would be able to look out and see the horizon, the curvature of the earth. I would like you to think about this: is the horizon a real physical thing, a location, or is it just a construct in our minds? Can you ever reach the horizon? Of course you can't. It just keeps moving away from you and you don't ever seem to be making any progress toward it or to be getting any closer to it. However, if you looked behind you at the shoreline that you left, you would be able to see that you really are making progress in the right direction as the shoreline recedes in the distance.

Sometimes our big goals, our "WHY" can seem much like the horizon. We know it's out there. We really do want to 'get there'. But on a day-to-day basis it may not seem like we are making any real progress toward our goal.

It is very important to break our big goals down into daily activity goals that we know are necessary to make progress and move forward. We can measure our daily activities. We can see that we are doing the "right things" to achieve our big goal. We can in fact see that we are making progress and moving in the right direction.

It's not enough to only have the big goal. We need to identify the specific steps required to get there so that we can measure our progress. We will spend more time on this when we get to the section on creating your plan. (Chapter 18)

RAS: Question #3
Does it match my version of "the truth"?

The third question the RAS constantly asks is, "Does it match my version of the truth?" It is our version of the "the truth" (our self-image, our current PERCEIVED reality) that creates our limiting beliefs and 'bad maps'. The only way we can begin to permanently alter our behavior is to raise our self-image (Law #6). We need to start 'practicing our future perfectly'. Law #5 says, "Our self-image can be changed through clear, specific, vivid, emotional experiences, *whether real or imagined.*" We are going to begin to create those 'perfect' experiences through the use of afFORMations and aligning our self-talk with our afFORMations and goals. When we then learn how to combine all of that with Mental Contrasting (coming in chapter 16) we will have the ability to dramatically change the direction of our lives.

First, this is where we must take ownership of our thought life – to intentionally focus on those things that are important to us (our goals) and to develop the discipline to control our self-talk to be in alignment with our goals. There is a verse about not "putting new wine into old wine skins." We can't put new goals into our lives with old mind-sets. It just won't work. We need new thinking when we set new goals.

Part of taking responsibility for our lives and our futures, is to take responsibility for our thoughts and our words. We need to pay attention to what we are thinking about. We need to think about what we think about! – That's what is called metacognition today – thinking about what you are thinking about..

Proverbs 25:28 says, "A man without self-control is as defenseless as a city with broken-down walls." We must begin to have the self-discipline to take control of our thought life and our words. If we expect to change, it all starts here:

Romans 12:1-2 "I am being transformed by the renewing of my mind." Notice that this verse says the <u>renewing</u> of the mind. To renew is not to make different, not to replace it with something else, but to return it to its original state or original form. In other words, we are being transformed by bringing our minds back to what they were originally in Christ before we let the 'world' mess it up.

Be sure to spend some time with the affirmations of who God said we are in the next section. Also, dwell on these verses:

2Corinthians 5:7 "I am not moved by what I see. "

2Corinthians 10:4-5 "I am casting down vain imaginations. I am bringing every thought into captivity. "

It is time to start thinking about and taking ownership of what we think about!

INSIGHTS: "We have to have clear, specific and measurable goals."

"So much truth in this chapter I will have to go over it many times. I have always thought I had set goals but not the way I should. Setting a goal and keeping focused on that goal is HUGE. I always say I want to do something and then just trust God it will happen if it's in His will. Then I would figure when it failed that it wasn't supposed to be. This chapter changes everything. I'm like your granddaughter, Kristina, I don't keep my eye on the goal I keep my eyes on my feet so I don't fall. I stay safe but never achieve much."

"Your goals must be: WRITTEN - CLEAR- SPECIFIC- MEASURABLE or you will stay stuck."

Chapter 15
FORMING YOUR BETTER FUTURE

AfFIRMing or AfFORMing our better futures?

Virtually every goal setting and motivational seminar I ever attended for 30 years emphasized the need to do af**FIRM**ations in order to achieve my goals. Many times I spent weeks if not months very diligently doing what I was taught with no significant changes or results. What I have experienced doesn't track with what I was taught.

For example I would get up in the morning and spend a few minutes af**FIRM**ing my better future: "I have abundance. I have more than enough. I am financially free." Over and over and over again. Then I would look at the stack of unpaid bills on my desk and that still, small voice (my self-talk) was saying: "Yeah, right! Who are you trying to kid? You haven't ever been able to pay all your bills on time. It's never going to happen. You know you will always be broke. I mean really. You thought you would get there last month, but noooooooooooooo the dishwasher has to break and be replaced last week. It doesn't matter how hard you try there will always be something that screws it up!"

I found that whenever I affirmed something – a goal – that was way out in the future, way beyond my current reality, my self-talk would kick in and merely af**FIRM** the reality that I was stuck in at the moment. There is a very important place for af**FIRM**ations in our lives because there is one thing we do have control over – our actions and activities. We will come back to this when we talk about "TRIGGERS". (See the next Chapter)

One of the more important things for us to recognize is that our conscious mind is capable of thinking about and seeing both the future and the past. ***BUT our nonconscious mind only responds to 'right now'.***

As we profess to claim our better future by doing af**FIRM**ations with our conscious mind – our nonconscious mind continues to affirm who and what we are right now – our current perceived reality. The nonconscious continues to focus on our limitations, our weaknesses, our failures. Since 90% of the decisions and choices we make are made by our nonconscious mind without any conscious awareness it can often be a losing battle. So might there be something we can do that will keep us from having to do constant battle with our 'now self' – our current perceived reality?

When we make a statement (af**FIRM**ation) that is not yet true (especially if it is waaaaaay beyond our current reality) we encounter resistance – our negative self-talk. However, when we ask a question there is no resistance. Empowering questions cause your mind to focus on what you **HAVE** instead of what you **LACK**.

Dolores Albarracin and Ibraham Senay of the University of Illinois and Kenji Noguchi of the University of Southern Mississippi conducted a series of experiments demonstrating the difference between making positive declarative statements (af**FIRM**ations) about one's performance versus asking questions of oneself (af**FOR**Mations). They gave a group of people a series of puzzles to solve. One minute before they started half of the people were told to affirm to themselves that they would be able to solve the puzzles. The other half were told to ask themselves if they would solve the puzzles.

The group that asked themselves about their success solved 50% more puzzles than the half that declared (af**FIRM**ed) that they would. In a whole array of different types of experiments they consistently found that people who ask themselves appropriate questions outperformed those who pumped themselves up with positive af**FIRM**ations.[Senay, Albarracin, Noguchi, "Motivating Goal-Directed Behavior Through Introspective Self-Talk: The Role of the Interrogative Form of Simple Future Tense", *Psychological Science* 21, no.4 (April 2010) 499-504]

It turns out your mind has a powerful search function – think of it like Google. **When you ask yourself a question, your mind automatically searches for an answer.** (Psychologists call this "*embedded presupposition factor.*") This is like having a secret decoder ring that actually works. When you ask yourself the right kind of question, *your mind will begin to search for the answer,* ***which means that it will look for all of the strengths, talents and power that you can bring to the party.***

Noah St. John came up with the concept of Af**FORM**ations: empowering questions that cause your mind to begin to search for the answers that will help you focus on your strengths instead of your weaknesses. [In his book, *"Afformations: The Miracle of Positive Self-Talk"* you can expand on this concept if you wish]

James 4:2 is a verse that I have heard for years: "You do not have because you do not ask." I can't help but wonder if it is referring to asking ***ABOUT*** things and not just asking ***FOR*** things…

Instead of your self-talk sounding like this: "I am so uncomfortable around strangers. I really don't want to go to that mixer. Nobody ever talks to me. It's just too hard meeting new people and getting them to like me."

What if you were to ask yourself: "Why am I becoming more comfortable around strangers?" Your nonconscious mind (like your Google search engine) goes to work to answer the question and consciously you begin to register: "Because I've learned to ask open-ended questions and keep the focus on them. Because I've learned to really listen to what they say instead of thinking about what I'm going to say so they know I am really interested in them. Because I've learned to keep my body language more open so that they are comfortable and open...." You will begin to focus on what you want instead of what you don't want. (Remember the strength test: "Don't drop the arm." vs. "Steel rods, power and strength."

Instead of: "Who are you trying to kid? You haven't ever been able to pay all your bills on time. It's never going to happen. You know you will always be broke. I mean really. You thought you would get there last month, but nooooooooooooo the dishwasher has to break and be replaced last week. It doesn't matter how hard you try there will always be something that screws it up!"

What if you were to ask yourself: "Why are my finances improving every month?" Your nonconscious mind goes to work and you begin to consciously register: "Because I am disciplining my credit card use. I am able to put away a bit each month into an emergency fund. I am putting in extra overtime at work to build up a cushion...."

Using afFORMations makes conscious and clear that which has, until now, been only nonconscious and hidden. Empowering questions cause your mind to focus on what you have vs. what you lack. **Like the strength test that we do in live seminars demonstrates – it causes you to focus on what you DO want instead of what you DON'T want!**

INSIGHTS: "Empowering questions cause your mind to focus on what you have vs. what you lack."
"I really like the idea of AfFORMations. Using questions really does activate the use of the brain better and listening to the answer allows me to learn more about what I am capable of."
"Start asking yourself questions like you ask Google."
"Take some time writing 5 afFORMations related to your top goals."

Chapter 16
IF THE GLASS IS HALF FULL
WHY AM I STILL EMPTY?

Gabriele Oettingen in her book *"Rethinking Positive Thinking"* presents a wealth of recent research that indicates *Positive Thinking* is absolutely necessary, but not sufficient for people to achieve their goals and dreams. (I would encourage you to read her book…)

In a previous chapter where we talked about affirming something out in the future and far beyond where our current reality is, our nonconscious mind and self-talk tend to dredge up all the reasons why we can't or we won't ever reach that goal. We have to work to achieve our goals in the real world with all its challenges, interruptions, obstacles and barriers – not in some airy-fairy make believe world that we wish would exist. When we visualize and think positively about our desired goals, for a short period of time we can convince our nonconscious minds that we are already there. Well, if we are already there why do we need to DO anything to get there?

There is a fascinating study among many others that shows: "While visualization can help us create a picture of the desired goal and its outcome, by itself it doesn't help us fulfill needs that require significant energy, effort or commitment. Positive visualization hinders us in handling hard tasks but spurs us to perform easy tasks." ["Needs Instigate Positive Fantasies of Idealized Futures", *European Journal of Social Psychology* 42 (2012) 299-307]

It turns out that people who ONLY think positively about and visualize their goals and their futures do not act on those goals as much as someone who thinks about their goals in the context of their current reality with the obstacles and challenges they have to deal with in their everyday lives: "Using brain imaging responses to mental contrasting showed *enhanced activity* in sections of the brain responsible for willfulness, memory, and more vivid holistic thinking – a much different pattern when people are in their normal resting state or when they are merely visualizing about their desired future." ["Strategies of Intention Formation Are Reflected In Continuous MEG Activity", *Social Neuroscience* 4 (2009): 11-27]

In other words, unless we think about our goals in contrast to the challenges, frustrations, obstacles and barriers that occur in our everyday lives we are not as likely to take the action necessary to achieve those goals. Gabriele Oettingen calls this "Mental Contrasting".

Do You Really Want To Think About Everything That *Can Go Wrong?*

Emergency Procedures
When I was taking flight training, we spent what I thought was an inordinate amount of time in Ground School before ever setting foot in an airplane. I just wanted to get into the plane and fly. It turns out there are a few important things one must learn before getting into an airplane – like what keeps it up in the air for starters (besides the engine).

A significant part of ground school was studying and memorizing emergency procedures. It is important to understand all of the things that can go wrong, and know what to do if it should happen. Airplanes have a nasty habit of falling out of the sky if you do the wrong thing in an emergency. I didn't memorize all of the things that could go wrong and what to do about them in hopes that I would get to use that knowledge. But it gave me a significant comfort level knowing that I was prepared.

The most important lesson to be learned is that regardless of anything else that is going on, you must "fly the plane." Now that may seem patently obvious to you, but when things start going wrong in the cockpit, it is very easy to get so distracted by the problem that you are not paying attention to actually flying the plane. That's when most accidents happen. When things start to go wrong and you lose sight of your goal, it is very easy to "crash and burn."

The first time I ever took my wife up at night – who was petrified to start with – we hadn't been in the air five minutes when the whole electrical system died – no radio, no lights, no navigation system. How do you think she would have handled the situation if I had said, "Listen honey, under your seat is this big, thick pilot's manual. Would you pull that out and look in the index for 'Electrical System, Failed' and see what it says I'm supposed to do now"? She would have had a coronary on the spot. But since I had memorized the emergency procedures, I had it diagnosed and back on line before she even realized there was anything very serious going on. We will always be more effective, when we anticipate the things that may go wrong.

Plan B

As an aerospace engineer I was involved in several of the early and exciting space programs. Skylab – the first-ever space station, the Viking Lander on Mars, early Shuttle programs, the first capture and repair of an ailing satellite, and the design of the Manned Maneuvering Unit – the jet-propelled backpack that the astronauts fly around in space with.

One of my jobs was to conduct what was called a "Failure Mode and Effects Analysis." Basically, it entailed dreaming up anything and everything that could go wrong --from hardware failures to something as simple as an astronaut flipping switches in the wrong order. It was critical to try and anticipate anything that could put an astronaut's life at risk.

I called it the "What If?" game. "What if this happens? What if that happens? What if that happens before this? What if this never happens at all?" I tried to exhaust every possibility ahead of time. Then we created a 'fix' ahead of time, so that the astronauts didn't have to sit around scratching their heads, trying to figure out what to do next. It was important that they spend as little time as possible in life-threatening situations.

In many cases it meant building more redundancy into a system so that there were backups in case of a failure, but more often it meant pre-defining a set of procedures to get them back on track – a Plan B. And as someone recently reminded me, if Plan A doesn't work there are 25 more letters in the alphabet. ☺

Murphy

So what has all of that got to do with your plan? It was Robert Burns that penned the line, "The best laid plans of mice and men gang aft aglee." In other words, our plans often go astray. "Murphy's Law" says if anything CAN go wrong – it WILL go wrong. Unfortunately, Murphy has a nasty habit of showing up at the most inopportune times.

No matter how well you plan, you won't anticipate everything that can happen. In addition, right from the start you know there will be things that conspire against you accomplishing everything you set out to do. When things go wrong, instead of sitting there scratching your head, it would be much better to have thought through the most common challenges and already have a contingency plan in place. You won't be stopped for nearly as long, and you'll get back on track without losing so much momentum.

Think about Nehemiah. He set out to rebuild the wall of Jerusalem. When King Artaxerxes asked Nehemiah, "For what do you make a request?" Nehemiah had a very clear and specific goal. He told the king how long it would take him and exactly what he needed to accomplish the task. He had a well-defined plan that took a whole chapter in the Bible to describe. He enlisted the other stakeholders, painted them into the vision and got their buy-in. Nehemiah 2:17-18 "Then I said to them, 'You see the trouble we are in, how Jerusalem lies in ruins with her gates burned. Come, let us build the wall of

Jerusalem, that we may no longer suffer disgrace.' And I told them of the hand of my God which had been upon me for good, especially the privileges that the king had given me. And they said, 'Let us rise up and build.' So they prepared themselves for the work ahead."

Nehemiah did it all just right. But that didn't mean that the plan would be executed flawlessly and without challenges. In fact they had to build with their tools in one hand while they held their weapons in the other in anticipation of an attack by Sanballat and Gesham. During the building of the wall Nehemiah had to endure ridicule, threat of attack, discouragement, whining of the people, compromise, slander and fear. In fact it took three chapters to describe all the problems and challenges. But he did get the wall built!

Hopefully you never encounter all that Nehemiah did in the pursuit of your goals, but know there will always be challenges. Be prepared. Plan ahead. Have a contingency plan. Above all, stay focused on your goal. "Fly the plane!"

"MENTAL CONTRASTING"

In *Rethinking Positive Thinking*, Gabriele Oettingen shares a preponderance of research that demonstrates that those people that:

---

1) Visualize and think positively about their **G**oals and

2) Visualize what the ideal **O**utcome will look like when achieved, then

3) Identify any **O**bstacles that may stop them and finally

4) Determine ahead of time a **P**lan of how they will prevent, circumvent or overcome those obstacles are significantly more productive than those who just think positively about their goals.

In fact, quite often, just thinking positively about our goals can actually **prevent us** from doing the work that will help us achieve those goals.

Here are just a couple of research citations that indicate that positive thinking is necessary, but not sufficient to achieve our goals. In other words positive thinking and visualization are something we NEED to do but *ARE NOT ALL* WE NEED TO DO:

"While visualization can help us create a picture of the desired goal and its outcome, by itself it doesn't help us fulfill needs that require significant energy, effort or commitment. Positive visualization hinders us in handling hard tasks but spurs us to perform easy tasks." From: "Needs Instigate Positive Fantasies of Idealized Futures", *European Journal of Social Psychology* 42 (2012) 299

"Using brain imaging responses to mental contrasting showed enhanced activity in sections of the brain responsible for willfulness, memory, and more vivid holistic thinking – a much different pattern when people are in their normal resting state or when they are merely visualizing about their desired future." From: "Strategies of Intention Formation Are Reflected In Continuous MEG Activity", *Social Neuroscience* 4 (2009): 11-27

In essence it looks like this:

ACTUAL ACTIVITY LEVEL DIRECTED TOWARD GOAL

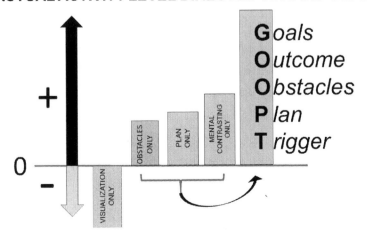

It is also interesting that the research points out people who just think about the obstacles and how to overcome them without significant focus on their goals are still more productive than those who just think positively about their goals. *WOW!*

It boils down to this: You will be much more effective when you 1) Define clear, specific, vivid, measurable goals 2) Visualize the desired outcome 3) THEN recognize the obstacles to achieving the goals 4) AND create a plan to overcome the obstacles 5) THEN **CREATE TRIGGERS FOR YOURSELF to make sure you execute the plan**

A "TRIGGER" is something you can af**FIRM** that you have 100% control over. So what is it that you have 100% control over? Your daily actions and activities. So instead of af**FIRM**ing something that is a long way from being yet real you can af**FIRM** something that is immediate and within your control NOW – the very activities that will move you toward your goal – the very activities that tend to get sabotaged by the real world in which you must function.

Remember that Step 3 in "Mental Contrasting" is to identify any obstacles that may stop you, distract you, sabotage you or get you off track. Step 4 is to create a plan in the context of the real life you are living with all of its challenges. TRIGGERS are a way to af**FIRM** the activities (that you have control over) required of your plan in juxtaposition to the obstacles and challenges you have every day of your life.

We will call these TRIGGERS "When – Then" scenarios or "If – Then" scenarios. You will discover that when you af**FIRM** these "Triggers" to yourself that they

> - **Remove ambivalence**
> - **Can turn negative situations into positives**
> - **Save energy**
> - **Help keep you focused (especially on "The ONE Thing")**
> - **Foster good habits**

> **Are most effective on hard-to-accomplish goals, not just the easy stuff**

Here is a template for creating "Triggers":

"When I encounter a specific situation [thought, person, visual cue, activity, challenge, obstacle, etc.], I will do the following [take a specific action, behave a certain way, say a certain thing, think a certain thought, etc.], so that I can achieve [the goal – "The ONE Thing"]."

Here are some examples:

> "When I get dressed and get to my desk the first thing I will do is write 3 follow-up notes/emails knowing it will help establish solid relationships with my customers." (As opposed to clicking on FaceBook and an hour and a half later, after having gone down 37 different rabbit trails wondering where the morning went…)

> "Before I do any household chores today I will call _____ to follow up." (Because I know that doing high-payoff activities are much more important than the laundry…)

> "When I get ready to go for my walk, I will first put together 5 follow-up mailings before I leave the house." (Knowing that having done so I can enjoy my walk without feeling guilty that I haven't worked on my goals yet today…)

> If when I get home from work I am too tired to go for a run I will at least put on my running shoes and step outside."

> "When I see _____ at the volleyball game today, I will ask enough questions to find out if there is something my product/service can help do to alleviate some challenges for her."

> ➤ "When I walk through the door to my chamber mixer this evening, I will immediately walk up to someone I don't know and introduce myself."

> ➤ "After the church service today, I will go to the fellowship hall and introduce myself to someone new."
> ➤ "If my spouse tries to heap guilt on me this evening when I need to invest some time in my home-based business I will ask to sit down and revisit our goals and afFIRM with him why it is important to achieve our financial goals."

> ➤ "If John comes into my office today for his usual 20-minute bull session I will politely afFIRM the importance of the quarterly report that we both have due on Friday."

The essence of all of this is pretty simple. Using the **GOOPT** strategy, in addition to visualizing our goals and the desired outcome, if we will identify those things that could prevent us from engaging in the productive activities that will move us toward our goals and create a plan how we will prevent or circumvent those obstacles and afFIRM the activities to move us forward ("Triggers") we are much more likely to 'succeed' than if we don't.

In fact there is a significant body of research that indicates we are 2-3 times more likely to accomplish the high-payoff activities by doing this than if we don't! But it is not only important to do these in the context of the obstacles and challenges we face but also in the context of things we do every day that can trigger a more productive activity leading toward our goals.

INSIGHTS: "Plan for Obstacles."

"I try to always be positive but the 'positive thinking' mantra drove me a little nuts. It was just positive 'Pie in the sky' thinking while doing nothing. Positive that you are waiting on God's will for your life. You have explained it very well here about thinking positive yet working that into our 'now'."

"Fly the plane" & create "TRIGGERS"

"GOOPT; make a copy and post in your workspace."

"Spend time looking at some of the obstacles and ask yourself 'how can I get through ____?' Write down the answers that come quickly to mind. Take 1 easy goal and work through the "GOOPT" process."

Chapter 17
THE SELF-TALK STRATEGY

We will not only reap what we sow, we will also reap more than we sow. Our words are the seeds and our heart (nonconscious mind) is the soil. Not only are the words we verbalize sown into our hearts, but the words that are part of the ongoing conversation we have with ourselves are also sown into our hearts (repetition, repetition, repetition!). In Chapter 10 we discovered the power of our words; how they are a reflection of our self-image as well as having a lot to do with the formation of our self-image.

It is critical to recognize that our self-talk is a reflection of what we truly believe about ourselves. Until our self-talk aligns with and supports our goals it will continue to work against us and sabotage our efforts at change.

Deuteronomy 30:15-19 "... I have set before you life and death, blessing and curse; therefore choose life, that you and your descendants may live, loving the Lord your God, obeying His voice and cleaving to Him....."

As we talked about in the beginning of this book, our life is all about choices. We all have free will, but God has made it abundantly clear that it is our responsibility to make the right choices, and one of those choices is to take responsibility for our self-talk. God seems to think what we say is important:

Proverbs 12:14 "From the fruit of his lips [his words] a man is filled with good things as surely as the work of his hands rewards him." What is just as important as the work? The words!

Mark 11:23 "For verily I say unto you, that whosoever shall say unto this mountain, be thou removed and be thou cast into the sea; and shall not doubt in his heart (nonconscious), but shall believe that those things which he saith shall come to pass; he shall have whatsoever he saith."

Knowing how dramatically our words affect us, it's imperative to take ownership of the words we speak and use. Begin to monitor what comes out of your mouth. When you detect something negative, when you hear yourself beating up on yourself, you have got to take the initiative to turn it around. You need to assure that your self-talk is in alignment with your goals, because your constant repetition of negative self-talk will perpetuate your low performance, sabotaging your desired goals. So how do we begin to fix it?

The first problem you are up against is that negative self-talk can be so natural, so much a part of how you have behaved your whole life, that you don't even recognize that it is negative. You can be blind to it. And what is the problem with a blind spot? You can't see it! So if you can't even see it, if you are not aware of it, how in the world are you supposed to fix it?

For many people, it is easier to spot negative self-talk coming out of someone else. When you hear someone else dumping on themselves, ask yourself, "Do I say that too?" Quite often you will discover that you do. Also, ask somebody that you respect and that is on the same page when it comes to this subject, to point out to you when they hear you saying something negative. The first step in fixing it is to become aware and to identify it. This really is crucial to our growth and change. Remember, "…..above all that you guard, watch over your heart, for out of it come the issues of life." Your self-talk is constantly planting seed in your heart (nonconscious). Are you planting the right kind of seed?

The Fix

When you spot negative self-talk, your immediate response should be to ASK AN EMPOWERING QUESTION. For example, if you hear yourself saying, "Sure enough, you messed it up again. You do that all the time. You are such a screw-up." – Your immediate response should be, "Why am I becoming a more competent and confident person? Why am I looking forward to the next opportunity to try that again?"

We learn by repetition and we can change through repetition. (Law #5) The thing that is repeated the most is our self-talk. It is imperative that it be supportive of the future we would like to create.

Hebrews 11:1 says, "Now faith is the substance of things hoped for, the evidence of things not seen." It is referring to the future that we have not yet achieved. Many people look at that verse and think that faith is some magical thing that is difficult to have or attain. But no one is faith*less*. It has nothing to do with whether or not we have faith. It is strictly a matter of what we put our faith in.

Our self-talk is a measure of where we place our faith. If we have faith that we always have and always will fail – we will fail. If we have faith that we aren't comfortable around other people – we won't be. If we have faith that we can never have a fulfilling, loving, and Christ-centered relationship – we won't. But we can also have faith in becoming the person we want to become – and we will.

Is It Faith or Is It Presumption?

I want to caution you at this point. Our words are powerful and compelling. Our self-talk is not only a reflection of how we see ourselves, but also one of the tools of change in our lives. The intent should be to become the person that God wants us to be. We should be immersed in God's word and focused on hearing God's will for our lives. We know from His word that when our will is aligned with His, He will give us "the desires of our hearts."

We're not talking here about 'name it and claim it." This is not the "God is my ATM" syndrome. Don't rush out ahead of God and demand results. Don't try to put God in a box and tell Him how He is supposed to accomplish your goals for you. But if we are in God's will, we can verbalize our faith, leaving the results in God's hands.

The overarching reason for controlling our self-talk is to center our thoughts on the nature and character of a faithful God. We are to affirm who we are in Him. (Whenever this becomes hard for you to do it is time to ask an empowering question to refocus on your strengths and your skills.) Our self-talk is a tool for us to change our emotions and our behavior, not to place God at our beck and call.

OK. Now go back and reread the previous four paragraphs about six times!

"I'm Lying To Myself"

Once we have the right perspective about self-talk, we're still not quite out of the woods. When we start to verbalize the person we want to become, but are not yet, it can sound "phony", feel uncomfortable and even seem like we are just lying to ourselves. We can begin to argue from our old, negative self that there is no way we can ever become or do what we are affirming. New words and patterns may feel uncomfortable at first, but so was learning to drive a stick-shift car. It was uncomfortable and unfamiliar, but after you learned it just became part of your repertoire and now you do all of it nonconsciously. Now it is comfortable. Just keep at it and you will find that new, positive self-talk will also become comfortable over time.

"It Didn't Stick"

I know many people that have worked on improving their self-talk for a while then stopped and got frustrated because the changes weren't "happening fast enough." It would be like someone going to the gym a few times, quitting, and then wondering why they didn't get or stay in shape. Exercise has to be a life-long endeavor if we are going to stay in shape. It would be like saying, "I ate yesterday. I don't understand why I have to eat today." The body has to be fed continually if we are to maintain our health. Our mind, our heart (nonconscious mind) also has to be fed continuously. Understand, this is a life-long discipline. Changing and improving your self-talk is not a one-time event – it is for life.

People quit because of 'failure', discouragement or pain. It hurts after exercising, so we stop exercising. We quit taking our vitamins because we caught the flu. We quit our positive self-talk because we didn't see immediate changes.

Think of it this way: What if you had a glass of filthy, dirty water and you put it under a faucet that was dripping – about one drop every hour. If you came back in a few hours or even a few days, you might not notice any change. You wouldn't see that the water had improved. But given a sufficient amount of time, you would come back and see a clean glass of water. In the near term, the changes were imperceptible, but in the long term the changes were dramatic.

We must have the patience and the faith that the change will come. Stick with it. Form these new disciplines in your life, and you will be rewarded.

Are You WILLING?

It takes time, effort and discipline to bring our thoughts and our words into subjection – but that day will come -- just continue to do what you know you should do. Are you WILLING to change? I want you to think of WILLING as a verb as well as an adjective. Not just, "Yes, I want to change." but also, "I am willing to change", meaning, "I choose to change", as an act of my will "I will do whatever I need to do to change." If you are willing to change, your better future is coming.

INSIGHTS: "Change is a life-long thing."

"Thank you for clarifying that what you are teaching us is not the 'Name It and Claim It' mantra that is out there. After dealing with low self-esteem for over 50 years, I hope I can deal with what my NONconscious is doing in my life. Our business is proof that all you have said is true. In 2009 my husband and I joined and lost about 30 pounds each, were involved in our group, achieved to Director in about 1 year and were even Star Achievers at the Washington DC Conference. Then all kinds of things happened to make me use excuse after excuse to show why I couldn't do a business, was tired of rejection and on and on. I proved myself right when we lost our Directorship after 8 months. I sunk into such a slump that we both gained all the weight back. This book has been a game changer!"

"We learn by repetition. Our words are POWERFUL - CHOOSE to CHANGE!"

"Monitor what comes out of your mouth this week. Replace negatives with a question (AfFORMation)."

Chapter 18
YOUR PLAN... BETTER YET –
DO YOU EVEN HAVE ONE?

Take a piece of paper and write down what you think you are worth on an annual basis – your goal, your dream. (No constraints, sky's the limit, if everything worked out just the way you think it should – what do you think you are worth?). Now that you are this far in the book, it should be easy for you. Go ahead, do it. Don't continue reading until you have written down a number............

Now, under that number, write down what you currently earn. I've got some bad news for you. The second number you wrote down – that's what you are worth. Do you hate that? You should hate that! It's not enough that you have a goal. You must also have a plan to achieve that goal. You need to know what is required to get there. You must know what activities and changes are required on your part in order to achieve your goal. Then you must be willing to commit to those activities.

I've seen countless people that have attended a goal-setting seminar or read a book on goal-setting and somewhere along the line they were taught that if you just write your goals down and stick them in a drawer, somehow all 'the powers of the universe' will come together to make it happen for you. I'm not going to try to argue the validity of that philosophy, but it should be fairly apparent that if you have a specific plan to achieve your goal, it is more likely to happen and to happen sooner.

Here is the point: You are worth whatever you think you are worth, IF you have the goal, A PLAN TO ACHIEVE IT AND ARE WILLING TO COMMIT. If you have the goal, but no plan, you are worth what you earn. If you know where you want to go, but don't have a clue how to get there, you're as good as stopped from the get-go. This income example was an easy one to use, but realize that this is true of any of your goals – whether it's related to your marriage relationship, your teenage kids, your community work or your spiritual walk. You need to have a clear, specific, vivid and measurable goal, but that in and of itself is not enough. You need to identify where you are right now in relationship to your goal, and what is going to be required of you to achieve it. Wanting to change isn't enough. You also need to come to grips with what specifically has to change.

To create an effective plan for reaching a goal requires four things:

1) Knowing exactly where it is you want to go, where you want to end up, and what that is going to look like when you have achieved it. (How you will measure 'success'.)

2) Knowing where you are right now in relationship to the goal.

3) Knowing what you are going to have to do and how you are going to get there – the activities required. (THE PLAN)

4) Be willing to commit.

Many people tend to skip number two, because it can be uncomfortable to acknowledge how far short of the goal we fall. But, think about it this way: Suppose you are going on a road trip; you can know exactly where you want to go and you can have the best and most accurate map in the world, but if you don't know where you are on the map, the map is worthless! On the other hand, if you have no map or a poor map (#3 above) you are again reducing your probability of 'success', of ever getting where you want to go.

At the same time that you are creating and acting on your plan (the specific activities required to achieve your goal) you also need to be working on yourself – your self-image – changing from the inside out. Remember – "Best you become a 'millionaire' before you get your million bucks, or you can't keep it!" Best you come to see yourself as a caring, thoughtful, considerate and helpful husband as you read the books, go to the marriage seminars and attempt to change your behavior, or you will revert right back to your old 'comfortable' patterns.

You may be beginning to feel that all of this is a very tall order to fill, but don't despair. It's all accomplished with simple steps that anyone can do if they choose to do them.

So what does an effective plan look like?

The Plan

For a plan to be effective, it should include:
➢ The specific activities and actions required to achieve the goal
➢ The frequency of each activity: Is it something you do once? Daily? Weekly? Monthly?
➢ Is there an end date for the activity or is it a new discipline you are developing for the rest of your life
➢ Identify how you will measure 'success' for each activity – how will you know when you have accomplished it?
➢ Identify any critical dates by which the activities need to be accomplished
➢ Be very specific about how much, how many, how soon, etc.
➢ Establish the amount of time you anticipate dedicating to each activity – is it 5 minutes per day, 10 hours per week, etc.
➢ Where do you need to fit each activity into your schedule in order to complete it in a timely fashion?
➢ ***Create "Triggers" for those important activities to increase your likelihood of doing them***
➢ Identify other stakeholders and how your activities will affect them. Communicate!
➢ With other stakeholders, create an "Expectations and Obligations" sheet. In other words, sit down and talk about

what you expect from each other in the way of support or help, and also what you obligate to each other in return. There is no need to have someone else sabotaging your efforts because you didn't communicate – it could be your spouse resenting the extra time you are putting into your new goals; it could be your kids making you feel guilty because you changed the schedule or expect them to help with the dishes in the evening in order for you to have more time to dedicate to your goals. Whatever it is, you need to communicate with the other stakeholders, so that they understand what your goals are, how they will be affected when you succeed and what the payoff is for them. Your life will be much easier if you have buy-in from them.

I've often heard it said that truly effective people spend an hour planning for every three to four hours of execution. Whether or not the numbers are accurate, the point is well taken: effective planning dramatically increases our effectiveness and our efficiency.

INSIGHTS: "Must have a plan and execute it."

"Make a plan and work the plan, be accountable to others all the while working on the positive retraining of my RAS, create triggers and stop letting my negative NONconscious win."

"Know where you are & where you want to go...HAVE A PLAN & be willing to commit."

Chapter 19
SELF-MANAGEMENT:
DO YOU HAVE TIME
FOR YOUR BETTER LIFE?

Let's start this chapter with the premise that ultimately your success will be about doing the right things, not doing everything right. "The main thing is to keep the main thing the main thing."

If you have gotten this far, you now have an excellent understanding of how to change yourself from the inside out and improve your performance. You know what your goals are. You also should have a well-defined plan to help you begin to meet the goals that you have set for your life. There's only one problem left to solve. Knowing that you have to live in the "real world" with all its responsibilities, demands and obligations, have you figured out if there is time for you to accomplish all that you profess to want to do? Could even Superman or Superwoman do it all?

At this point it would seem natural to discuss time management. But rather than doing that, it is more important to talk about self-management. It is always fascinating to see the people that read books, listen to CDs & Mp3s or attend seminars about time management, and yet very little ever changes for them. They learn a few tricks about being more efficient or getting more organized. But the real question is: efficient and organized for what? This most often occurs because they do not have clear goals that allow them to assess what the most important things are that they should be doing at any point in time. They haven't figured out "The One Thing."

Time management is not really about managing time – it is about managing ourselves and our priorities in the context of our goals. Time management outside the context of our goals is a waste of time. Without knowing exactly what you want and where you are going, whatever you choose to spend your time on is as good as anything else you might spend your time on – so what would be the point in "managing your time'?

Let's look at what self-management really is. The place to start is to figure out what your current obligations and responsibilities are. Put together a blank calendar of one week, with each day broken up into 30-minute increments. Begin by crossing off all the times that are currently committed to some activity or responsibility. For example, cross off the time you spend getting ready for work, meal times, your commuting time, time on the job, your prayer time, exercise time, family time, church activities, recreation, volunteerism, etc. In other words, take a snapshot of what your life and your days look like right now.

Next, look at your activity plan for each of your goals. Start fitting all of those additional activities required to reach your goals into your schedule. What do you discover as you do this? Do you find that you have more than enough time to accomplish your goals? If so, you are one of the fortunate few.

Most people find that there isn't nearly enough time to do everything that they are already committed to and then add all of the necessary activities to achieve their newfound goals. If that's the case for you, what do you do?

One of two things will have to happen. Either you will have to scale back your goals, or you will have to give up some of your current activities and commitments in order to make room for your new goals.

You have to decide which are the most important. Should your new goals take precedence over some of your existing activities and obligations? What are you willing to give up in order to achieve your goals?

Whichever is the "right" answer for you, it is very important that you schedule and put on your calendar, your 'smart phone, your "tickler file" or your "Day-Timer", those things that you have decided must get done. Create a calendar for your "ideal week" – the kind of week where you accomplish everything that you set out to do. Use that as your goal. You can't anticipate everything that may happen or when "Murphy's Law" is going to kick in, but you at least have a goal to shoot for, instead of just letting life happen to you.

What Are Your Priorities? What are your payoffs?

Too many people never go through the process of figuring out if they can actually fit everything they want to accomplish into their schedule, and as a result they are setting themselves up for failure and disappointment. There are very few people that can 'do it all'; given the time constraints and responsibilities they have in their lives. So one more time we are confronted with the importance of assessing our priorities – having to decide what the really important things to accomplish in our lives are. What is your "ONE THING" that requires your focus so that you will ultimately feel 'fulfilled' in your life?

It is essential at this point to make a couple of distinctions and give you a couple of definitions that will help you begin to figure all of this out. There is a significant difference between a priority and what we will call a "payoff". A PRIORITY is anything that you dedicate time to. A PAYOFF is any activity that moves you toward a valued goal. I doubt that you would ever admit to anyone that watching TV is a priority in your life. And yet, if you spend time watching TV, then by definition, watching TV is a priority in your life. Remember, a priority is ANYTHING you spend time on.

When you begin to evaluate how you are going to spend your time (and your life) it is important to make a distinction between PRIORITIES and PAYOFFS. Anything you do can fall into one of four different categories:

Category 1: High Payoff – High Priority
Category 2: High Payoff – Low Priority
Category 3: Low Payoff – High Priority
Category 4: Low Payoff – Low Priority

The key to a "successful" life is to learn to spend the majority of your time on Category 1 activities. The "One Thing" too often ends up in Category 2. Yes, it's a huge payoff but we don't commit time to it. We let all the Category 3 & 4 stuff get in the way.

Until we make the "One Thing" Category 1 and commit the time necessary to make it happen – nothing much will change in our lives. Unfortunately, 95% of the people spend most of their time on Category 3 & 4 activities because they are easy, they are routine and they require no risk. If we don't consistently commit time to high payoff activities – activities that will help us achieve our goals – we may check back next year or in five years and discover that our life hasn't changed. Just by virtue of the fact that you are reading this book tells me that you wouldn't want that to happen.

It is time to focus your time and your efforts on High Payoff activities – the "One Thing". It is imperative that you know what activities are required for every one of your goals.

Are You Guilty?

Assessing our priorities and payoffs, scheduling them and sticking to them helps solve another problem that a lot of people have. I've noticed that there are many people that spend most of their lives feeling guilty – mostly feeling guilty about whatever it is that they are NOT doing. If they are involved in some church activity, they are feeling guilty that they are not spending time with their kids. If they are spending time with the kids, they are feeling guilty that they are not spending time on the home-based business they are trying to start. If they are spending time on their business, they are feeling guilty that they aren't at the committee meeting for the non-profit they are involved in. And if they are working with the non-profit they are feeling guilty that they aren't at the church. No matter what they are doing, they feel guilty about whatever it is they are not doing.

In general, I think women are much more plagued by this vicious cycle of guilt than are men. Most men, if they have a 'TO DO' list for the day that has 5 items on it and they get three finished, they are really proud of themselves. If a woman has a 'TO DO' list of 87 items and she gets 86 done, she will feel guilty about the one she didn't finish, instead of feeling good about the 86 that she did finish!

One of the real values of knowing what our priorities and payoffs are, and scheduling them, is that when we are doing what we know we are "supposed to be doing", we don't have to feel guilty while we are doing it, because we know that the other important things are also on the calendar and will get their due at the appropriate time.

When I first had all the newfound freedom of not having to punch someone else's time clock, I thought that it would be great to not have a set schedule and to live 'spontaneously.' Much to my dismay, I accomplished very little and had no free time to do the recreational things I most enjoyed. It wasn't until I learned to schedule my time and stick to the appropriate priorities and payoffs that I had any free time for recreation, etc. And now, since I've learned to schedule my recreation, I can go and enjoy those activities without guilt, knowing the high payoff activities are also on the calendar.

How Often Do You Have a "Mrs. Furbie Attack?"

Another problem we can have by not knowing what our goals, priorities and payoffs are is what I call the Mrs. Furbie syndrome. Mrs. Furbie gets up in the morning and heads downstairs to make the kids' lunches for school before her husband gets up. On the way down the stairs she trips over the cat and realizes that she hadn't fed the cat last night, so she heads for the cupboard to get the cat food. As she reaches for the food, she sees the broom and it registers on her that she hasn't swept the kitchen floor for a couple of days. She grabs the broom and starts sweeping the kitchen when she hears her husband running the water upstairs and decides she had better get the coffee made. She puts the broom aside and starts making the coffee, but as she starts to get the water for the pot, her first child bounds down the stairs and says, "Good morning Mom. What's for lunch today?" Mrs.

Furbie realizes that she still hasn't made the lunches, so leaving the coffee half made, she heads for the refrigerator and when she looks inside she sees the leftovers from a week ago that now look like her teenager's science project. She grabs the leftovers and heads for the trash can in the garage to get rid of it and steps on the cat on the way out, realizing she hasn't fed the cat, she heads back to the cupboard to get the cat food............

Twenty minutes have passed and she hasn't made the lunches, made the coffee, swept the kitchen, fed the cat or accomplished anything else of "importance" yet that morning. Can you relate? What is Mrs. Furbie's problem? She has no sense of priorities or payoffs.

The Problem With "YES"

One of the challenges that many people have sticking to their plan is that they are missing a very crucial word in their vocabulary. That word is "NO." If you care about everyone else so much that whatever they request of you, your automatic response is "Yes", you will get so over committed and overwhelmed that you won't do a very good job at any of them, and certainly be distracted from those high-payoff activities that would move you toward your own valued goals. Too often "Yes" comes out of us before we have taken the time to evaluate whether or not we really have time to accomplish the request or if it even makes sense in the context of trying to achieve our goals.

When we get too over committed it is not unusual to let other people down, because there isn't enough time to do the job well if we manage to get to it at all.

It would be better to form the habit of your automatic response being, "No, I am afraid I can't fit that into my life right now." If after evaluating the request, you decide that it is something that fits with your goals and schedule and you can do it and want to do it, you can always go back to them and volunteer. They will be thrilled that you went out of your way to make it happen for them.

Schedule only 80%

As you are putting your schedule together for the day, the week, the month - leave a few holes in your calendar – some 'slop time' – so that if something untoward happens and disrupts your high-payoff activities, you can put them back in your schedule later in the day or the week. If you have every moment of every day booked solid, when things go wrong, there is no way to compensate for them. Only schedule about 80% of your time. You will not feel so pressured and you will be able to recover from setbacks much easier.

INSIGHTS: "You have to MAKE time for your goals."
"Create a calendar for your "IDEAL WEEK" + FOCUS your efforts on HIGH PAYOFF activities."
"Boy this chapter had my NONconscious negative self-talk in a tizzy. Change really is going to be like the drips into that dirty water. Slow and steady will win the race."
"Look at the way you used your time this past week. Now look at the priorities and payoffs. What needs to change?"

Chapter 20
REPRISE – The 6 Laws

Before we tie it all together in the last chapter, remember that it always starts with your thinking. So let's review the six laws that affect your behavior:

Law #1   Everything you think about affects you.
Everything you <u>put</u> in your mind affects you.
Everything you <u>allow</u> into your mind affects you.
Everything you <u>expose</u> your mind to affects you.

Law #2   Your self-image was formed by CLEAR, SPECIFIC, VIVID, EMOTIONAL experiences and/or lots of repetition.

Law #3   Your performance will never exceed your self-image by very much or for very long.

Law #4   Your nonconscious mind (heart) does not know the difference between a real event and a vividly imagined one.

Law #5   Your self-image can only be <u>changed</u> by CLEAR, SPECIFIC, VIVID, EMOTIONAL experiences whether real or <u>imagined</u>. (See #2)

Law #6   When you raise your self-image your performance will increase.

95% of the time these laws are working against people instead of for them – just because they don't know or understand them. By virtue of the fact that you have gotten this far in the book, you now know how to make them work in your favor. It's all about your THINKING.

Let's refresh our memory of what Philippians 4:8 says about our thinking: "Finally, brethren, whatsoever things are true, whatsoever things are honest, whatsoever things are just, whatsoever things are pure, whatsoever things are lovely, whatsoever things are of good report; if there be any virtue, and if there be any praise, think on these things."

Proverbs 4:20-25 does an excellent job of crystallizing the essence of this book:

"My son, listen to my words; incline your ear to my sayings; let them not depart from your eyes; keep them in the midst of your heart; for they are life to those finding them and healing to all their flesh. Above all that you guard watch over your heart [your nonconscious mind]; for out of it are the sources of life. Put away from you a crooked mouth, and put far from you perverse lips; let your eyes look forward and your gaze straight ahead of you. Consider well the path for your feet and all your ways shall be sure."

Sadly, this does not describe most people. Unfortunately, this is how 95% of the people actually live it:

"My son listen to your own and other people's negative words; incline your ear to your feelings; keep your feelings in view all the time; keep your feelings in the midst of your heart; for they are death to your goals and sickness to your flesh. Above all that you do, be sure to allow all the junk of TV, newspapers and the circumstances around you into your heart; then out of it will come failure and death. Be sure to continue to speak negatives and unbelief in who you say you are and what you say you can do and have; keep your eyes looking back at your circumstances so that you can't focus on your future. Do not look at the path before you and you will be sure never to reach your goal."

Ouch! That hurt. Hopefully, by now you have a sense of what it takes to live the way Proverbs actually describes it. So now, let's put all the pieces together in one place. The last chapter will summarize the concepts, disciplines, tools, actions or activities that will allow you to begin creating your better future. The whole book has provided the justification for and the foundation for these small disciplines. Small in terms of what it takes you to do them – huge in terms of the outcome WHEN you do them.

INSIGHTS: "Everything we think, expose our minds to and say affect us."

"What am I to do when my husband really doesn't care if we succeed? Maybe changing myself will help him too."

"Be careful of what or who you listen to, watch, read or otherwise let into your mind...guard your heart & be one of the 5%."

Chapter 21
PUTTING IT ALL TOGETHER

Here are the major pieces that when working together will give you exceptional results:
You may want to hang a copy of this up somewhere you will see it often so that it causes you to think about those things that will help improve your future.

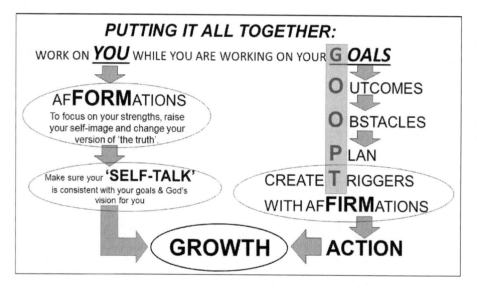

There are obviously three areas that need your time, your attention and your work. **YOU, your GOALS and YOUR LIFE.** Let's start with **YOU.** I've had a T-shirt for years that says: "For things to change, you have to change." I wore it for a very long time to remind myself because I need that reminder just as much as anyone else does.

YOU

The first thing you will want to do is get your RAS to open up so that you can see all the opportunities that surround you and probably have surrounded you all along. There are 3 things that have to happen for you to do that:

1. **Take responsibility for your life**. Now that you have completed this book, the future is your responsibility and God's and no one else's. Your RAS only opens up if it knows **you are RESPONSIBLE for the outcome**. (Chapter 10)

2. **Have CLEAR, SPECIFIC, VIVID, EMOTIONAL, *MEASURABLE* GOALS** so your RAS knows what is IMPORTANT and what you need to be aware of to get to your goals. (Chapter 14) **GOOPT** will help you do this.

3. **Change your version of "your truth"** – your self-image - your version of what you can do, cannot do, your strengths, your weaknesses, etc. **AfFORMations will allow you to focus on your strengths instead of your weaknesses. (Chapter 15) You must also align your SELF-TALK** with your goals and af**FORM**ations, but more importantly align your self-talk with who God says you are and who you are as a child of Christ. (Chapter 17)

YOUR GOALS

4. Surly old Curly is asking you right now: "What is your ONE THING?" Keep redoing the exercises in Chapter 14 until you figure it out. Get to the place where you have clear, specific, vivid, emotional, MEASURABLE **GOALS**.

5. Think about and visualize the ideal **OUTCOME** of that how you would like your life to be because of that goal.

6. Be realistic and identify the challenges, **OBSTACLES**, frustrations and barriers in this real life that you have to live – those things that distract you, sabotage you or keep you stuck - Whether they be current responsibilities, relationship issues, lack of self-esteem or anything else that continues to surface.

7. Create a **PLAN** to prevent, circumvent or fix those obstacles and challenges when and if they occur.

8. Create **TRIGGERS** for the specific activities that you identify in #7 that will move you forward.

YOUR LIFE

9. Take the time to create a calendar for an "ideal week" so that you know how to schedule your time to be more effective and to be sure you have the time to achieve your goals.

10. **Continuously monitor and measure your activities** to assure that you are on track toward your goals.

11. Find a mentor, a coach or a support group who is willing to tell you the truth and help you find your 'blind spots'. Be willing to be accountable to them. Tell them what your activities should be and allow them to ask if you have done them and allow them to critique your results.

Eleven things. Just eleven things that if you do them consistently, you will begin to move toward your desired future. You will become the person you want to become and the person God designed you to be. Eleven things that will allow you to begin living up to your full potential. Is your better future worth forming the small disciplines found in those eleven things? Is there anything on that list that you can't do or are not willing to do? Just eleven small disciplines. Eleven small disciplines that will help you begin to be a person that advances the Kingdom of God in powerful ways. Eleven small disciplines that will move you to be a 'minister in the marketplace'. Just eleven small disciplines. Amazing – only eleven – and they are easy to do at that.

As a reminder, it might be valuable to print out and post these eleven small disciplines above your desk or your computer or wherever you know you will see them often. You can do each one of them. None of them are insurmountable. The question is – will you?

You now have the tools. Will you use them? Or will you fall asleep on your toolbox? Are you going to put this book on the shelf to collect dust like so many other self-help books you've purchased? Or will you take these concepts to heart (literally) and make them work for you? I know you can. You must decide that you will.

INSIGHTS: "Commit your works to the Lord."

"You have shown me that God does have a plan for my life and it is to be successful. Money is not evil, only the love of money."

"Print out the 11 steps + Open your RAS & Commit your work to the Lord."

POSTSCRIPT

Some parting thoughts for you.

The Bible, the "Manufacturer's Handbook" should be your constant guide and source of inspiration. Joshua 1:8 says, "This book of instruction must not depart from your mouth; you are to recite it day and night so that you may carefully observe everything written in it. For then you will prosper and have great success."

I believe that "All truth is parallel." The Lord's Prayer says: "...thy kingdom come, thy will be done on earth as it is in heaven." On earth as it is in heaven. **On. Earth.** As. It. Is. In. Heaven.

James 1:22 says: "But be doers of the word and not hearers only, deceiving yourselves." You have read a lot of words in this book. You have gained some insights into how you can alter your behaviors and your future. You have some tools that can help you move forward. It's not enough to be hearers. Unless you apply what you have learned, unless you instill these small disciplines into your daily routines – nothing will change. "For things to change, you have to change." This is your time. You have what you need. *You bring lots to the party.* Invest it in yourself and then go out and invest in someone else's life. You can help change the world one person at a time. Be **THAT** person.

Proverbs 16:3 "Commit your work to the Lord and your plans will be established and succeed." Keep that perspective at all times!

ACKNOWLEDGEMENTS

Many people reviewed, commented and offered their insights as I was wrapping up this edition. Among them were Gary Burke, Gail Davis, Adona Driscoll, Linda Duvall, Zal Fink, Amy Hagerup, Lesley Huff, Debra Hugunin, Nancy Mitchell, Karen Palino, Bonnie Stacy, Paula Thomas, Tammy Taylor Woolard. Thank you all for your time and your thoughtfulness. May God bless each of you abundantly.

AFTERWORD

If you would like to host a full-day seminar covering this material contact:

Rick Seymour at 303-818-9798

Email: rickseymour@comcast.net

AFTER-AFTERWORD: "YOUR ONE THING"

If you have not yet found your "One Thing" and are looking for a financial opportunity, please visit: http://success.myshaklee.com
If it seems like a fit for you, please contact me and we can talk about your better future.

26708490R00096

Made in the USA
Middletown, DE
05 December 2015